초판 1쇄 인쇄	2014년 1월 6일
초판 2쇄 발행	2015년 11월 3일

지은이	송윤정, Crystal L. Hecht
발행인	김용부
발행처	글로벌문화원
주소	서울시 종로구 관철동 11-19 글로벌빌딩
전화	02) 725-8282
팩스	02) 753-6969
홈페이지	http://www.globalbook.co.kr
등록번호	제 2-407
등록일자	1987년 12월 15일

기획총괄	이경헌
편집	김지선
디자인	새힘
일러스트	양민희
제작	이재봉

ISBN 978-89-8233-202-9 13740

★이 교재의 내용을 사전 동의나 허가 없이 무단으로 복사, 복제, 전재하는 것은 저작권법에 저촉되며, 법적인 제재를 받게 됨을 알려 드립니다.

Copyright©2014 by Global Culture Center Co. All rights reserved.
First edition printed in 2014, Seoul, Korea.

Preface
머리말

길을 건너기 위해 신호등이 바뀌기를 기다리면서 폰을 들여다봅니다. 알림음과 함께 반가운 메시지가 눈에 들어옵니다. 입가에는 미소가 드리우고 곧이어 바쁘게 손가락이 움직입니다. 우리 주위를 둘러보면 이렇게 폰으로 누군가와 대화를 나누고 있는 모습을 흔히 볼 수 있을 것입니다. SNS(Social Networking Service)는 이미 이 시대에서 바쁘게 쫓기며 살아가는 현대인들을 이어주는 친숙한 의사소통 수단이 되었고, 이런 점에서 분명 언어 학습의 유용한 도구가 될 수 있을 것입니다. 한국과 같은 EFL(English as a Foreign Language; 영어가 외국어로 쓰이는) 상황에서 영어 학습자들이 SNS의 무한한 혜택을 받을 수 있다는 믿음으로 시작된 본 프로젝트에 운좋게도 저희 두 명의 저자가 공동으로 집필을 맡게 되었습니다.

교실수업에서 강의와 교재를 통해 이루어지는 영어학습은 영어를 모국어로 사용하는 원어민들이 실생활에서 사용하는 언어를 느끼고 호흡하는 데 있어 학습자들로 하여금 괴리감을 느끼게 합니다. 아마도 학습환경 그 자체가 어느 정도는 책임이 있지 않나 생각됩니다. 이제 교사와 학생들 간의 다소 어색함 속에서 '학습을 통해 이루어지는 콘텐츠'는 잠시 한켠으로 밀어 두고, 매일매일 일상 생활에서 흔히 만날 수 있는 친구, 언니, 형, 오빠, 누나 또는 동생과 같은 아홉 명의 주인공들의 이야기를 소개할까 합니다. 우리 주인공들이 엮어 내는 '모바일을 통한 진솔한 이야기'로 이 책의 독자들은 보다 현실적인, 그리고 현재 통용되는 다양한 영어 표현들을 익히게 될 것입니다. 물론 끊임없는 독자의 흥미를 자아내기 위해 다소 드라마틱한 요소도 포함되었답니다. ^^~
글을 쓰는 내내 한국적 정서와 문화 배경을 염두에 두었기때문에 독자들이 100개의 에피소드를 차례로, 또는 무작위로 읽어가면서 "이거야!" 하고 콕 짚으며 함께 공감하고 결국 그 영어 표현을 본인의 것으로 만들 수 있을 거라고 한껏 기대해 봅니다.

마지막으로 저희들의 오랜 염원을 담아 함께 글을 쓰고 독자와 교류할 기회를 주신 모든 분들께 고마움을 전하며, 특히, 글로벌문화원 임직원 여러분께 다시 한번 감사의 마음을 전하고 싶습니다.

저자 일동

구성과 특징 **Feature**

Chatter & Chitchat

일상생활, 비즈니스 등 8개의 장르(Chatter)와 100의 소재(Chitchat)로 구성, 주인공들의 재미있고 흥미진진한 에피소드와 애환, 가십거리 등을 담았습니다.

Chatting & Talking

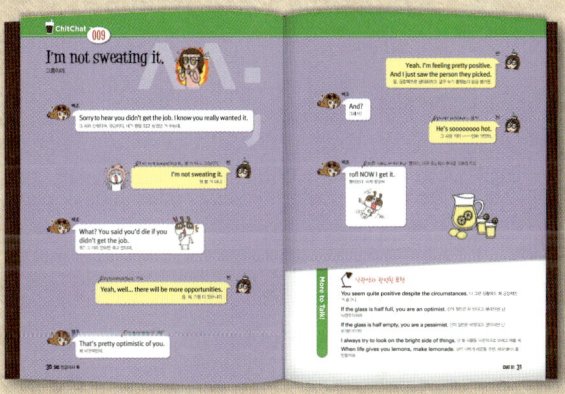

스마트폰 SNS 화면이 연상되는 다채로운 바탕에 주인공들의 대화를 실감나게 소개합니다. 특히 주인공의 성격을 대표하는 캐릭터 설정과 상황에 따른 다양한 컬러 삽화로 내용 이해를 돕고 표현 학습의 흥미를 북돋웁니다. More to Talk에서는 소재와 관련, 대체 가능하고 다채로운 추가 표현을 학습할 수 있도록 합니다.

Review

장르별, 소재별로 앞서 학습한 주요 표현들을 다시 복습할 수 있도록 정리, 실제 SNS 기반 영어 대화 및 실용 회화에 활용할 수 있도록 하였습니다.

Contents
차례

CHAT 01 Work & Career

001	It's now or never.	14
002	I can feel it in my bones.	16
003	You've got what they want.	18
004	This project is my baby.	20
005	I'm flat broke.	22
006	Been there, done that.	24
007	I'm in over my head.	26
008	It's a foot in the door.	28
009	I'm not sweating it.	30
010	YOLO(You Only Live Once)	32
011	It was a close call.	34
012	Working around the clock is a must to get ahead.	36
013	I owe you a big one.	38
014	I smell a rat.	40
	Review	42

CHAT 02 Appearance

015	You should call ahead for an appointment.	46
016	How about bangs?	48
017	I went a little too far…	50
018	I couldn't even recognize her!	52
019	I can't get rid of this backne.	54
020	You've got to look the part.	56
021	I have NOTHING to wear.	58
022	You look fresh off the runway.	60
023	Isn't it too showy for the first date?	62
024	I look like I just rolled out of bed.	64
025	What's your point?	66
	Review	68

CHAT 03 — Love

026	Love is one thing and marriage is another.	72
027	It's not like I have a ring on my finger.	74
028	She won't give me the time of day.	76
029	What's with you lately?	78
030	Pull yourself together.	80
031	It was a total disaster!	82
032	Epic fail	84
033	It's just not working.	86
034	Friendship between men and women is impossible. Period.	88
035	Two-timing is not my thing.	90
036	I made a faux pas.	92
037	He's still hung up on his ex.	94
	Review	96

CHAT 04 — Health & Food

038	Speak for yourself.	100
039	He lives off ramen and soda.	102
040	What exactly is that?	104
041	I'm not sure what she's into.	106
042	What should I eat to up my stamina?	108
043	I occasionally splurge on weekends.	110
044	The meat was dry and the veggies were all mushy.	112
045	Do they have any lo-cal options?	114
046	My stomach is growling.	116
047	What are you in the mood for?	118
048	You're hitting the gym pretty hard.	120
049	My head is killing me.	122
050	I'm quitting alcohol cold turkey!	124
051	I tripped while texting and walking.	126
052	My head feels foggy.	128
053	Worry can make you sick.	130
054	I'll keep my fingers crossed.	132
055	You'll be back to normal in no time.	134
	Review	136

 **Contents**

CHAT 05 Relationships

056	She's driving me up the wall.	140
057	I couldn't believe my eyes!	142
058	Just don't screw this up.	144
059	You've got it all wrong.	146
060	He's creeping me out	148
061	He's a total nightmare.	150
062	I'll make it up to you.	152
063	Things just aren't the same anymore.	154
064	Let me get back to you later	156
065	Your heart was in the right place.	158
066	We have a love-hate relationship.	160
Review		**162**

CHAT 06 Tech

067	My contract is up.	166
068	Just give it a go!	168
069	I'm having trouble figuring this thing out.	170
070	This is my last resort.	172
071	It's gonna blow your mind!	174
072	It's revolutionized my life!	176
073	It keeps turning off.	178
074	I shrank my entire wardrobe.	180
075	Who can keep track of all these accessories?!	182
Review		**184**

CHAT 07 Leisure Activities

076	Bored out of my mind.	188
077	I haven't gone anywhere in ages.	190
078	He's an athletic freak.	192
079	I'm drawn to baking classes.	194
080	Let's get together more often.	196
081	It was a waste of time.	198
082	No wonder you're so good at English!	200
083	That's my show!	202
084	Just the thought of it makes me cringe.	204
085	I feel like an entirely new person.	206
086	Where is your sense of adventure?	208
Review		**210**

CHAT 08 Everyday Life and Problems

087	What am I? Chopped liver?	214
088	Cutting food waste helps Korea go greener.	216
089	She never throws anything away.	218
090	I got caught jaywalking.	220
091	Just for kicks.	222
092	I'm already regretting it.	224
093	It's like the 7th solid day of rain.	226
094	Maybe he has some other issue.	228
095	Guys, bundle up.	230
096	Not in a million years.	232
097	I had my fortune told.	234
098	It cost me an arm and a leg.	236
099	She's a super haggler.	238
100	I'll have to eat and run.	240
Review		**242**

Reference Charts
영어 채팅 참고 자료

상황에 따라 매너있게, 또는 친근한 표현을 선택해서 쓸 수 있어요.

1. 격식 있는 표현 vs 친한 사이의 표현

Formal	↔	Informal
Good morning.	Hello. / Hi.	Hey.
Do you have time?	Are you busy?	U busy? / Busy?
Thank you.	Thanks.	Thanx / Thx
Could I call you later?	Can I call you later?	Call you later!
I'm looking forward to it.	Looking forward to it.	Can't wait!
Goodbye.	Bye.	Later.

2. 흔히 쓰이는 채팅 약어

lol, LOL	Laughing Out Loud	b/c	Because
lmao, LMAO	Laughing My Ass* Off	w/	With
rofl, ROFL	Rolling On the Floor Laughing	w/o	Without
U, u	You	XOXO	Hugs & Kisses
UR, ur	You're, Your	np	No Problem
R U, r u	Are you	Thx, Thanx	Thanks
Y	Why	TMI	Too Much Information
OIC, I C	Oh I See, I See	2nite	Tonight
OK, ok, K, k	Okay	2morro	Tomorrow
CU, See u	See you	GF	Girlfriend
OMG	Oh My God	BF	Boyfriend
OMF*G	Oh My F* God	BFF	Best Friend Forever
BTW	By The Way	ASAP	As Soon As Possible
Srsly?	Seriously?	SMH	Shaking My Head
NEway	Anyway	FYI	For Your Information
gtg, g2g	Got To Go	IMO	In My Opinion
BRB	Be Right Back	TY	Thank You
ttyl	Talk To You Later	W/B, wb	Write Back, 또는 Welcome Back
J/K, JK, jk	Just Kidding		

3. 흔히 쓰이는 줄임말 표현

Going + to = **gonna / gunna**	I'm gonna go tonight. U gonna go? / Gonna go?
Want + to = **wanna**	I wanna go out. U wanna..? / Wanna go out?
Got + to = **gotta**	I gotta go. / Gotta go.
Have + to = **hafta**	I hafta go. / Hafta clean my room.
Kind + of = **kinda**	I'm kinda busy. / Kinda busy.
Give + me = **gimmie**	Gimme a call later.
Don't + know = **dunno**	I dunno.
What + are+ you = **whatcha**	Whatcha doing?
Out + of = **outta**	I'm outta luck.

4. 영어 채팅에서 흔히 쓰이는 이모티콘

기쁨	:) :o) =)
신난다	:D :-D XD
윙크	;) ;-] ;D
언짢음	:/ :-/ >:\
슬픔	:(:-[
화남	>:(>:O
울음	:'(
메롱	:P :-p XP
황당함	:$:-$
할 말 없음	:-X

Characters
등장 인물 소개

천사표

다정한 성격의 소유자로 풀타임 주부이다. Kell2013의 절친이자 초등 동창으로 단 한번도 직장에 다녀본 경험이 없다.

Kell2013

독립적 성격의 일중독증세를 보이는 싱글녀이다. 친구들과 온라인/오프라인으로 수다를 떨면서 스트레스를 해소하려고 한다.

동분서주

똑부러지고 현실적인 성격으로 로펌에서 법률 비서로 일하는 싱글녀이다. 머리끝부터 발끝까지 자신을 가꾸길 좋아한다.

겜페남

아주 재미난 성격의 백수이자 컴퓨터 게임 매니아이다. 친구들은 그가 현실세계와 가상세계를 구분 못한다고 생각한다.

백조

쇼핑, 패션, 팝음악을 사랑하고, 패션잡지사에서 일하는 게 꿈인 싱글녀로 현재 몇 명의 남자와 데이트 중이다.

빈

일명 "Bean", 냉소적이지만 재미있는 성격을 가진 커피 중독자로 무의미한 데이트에 지친 그녀는 최근 직장 상사에게 약간 관심을 갖게 된다.

Jas

새로 시작하는 게임회사 사장으로 자신의 일에 열심이면서도 느긋하고 열린 마음의 소유자이다. 직업상 늘 여행을 한다.

King_Michael

명문가 출신으로 명문대에서 MBA 과정 중인 학생이다. 비즈니스와 금융, 재테크에 올인하며 Early Adopter로서 디지털 신제품 애호가이다.

Tae

회사원으로 축구, 농구, 야구를 즐기는 미국인이다. 싱글남이며 여행을 좋아한다.

CHAT 01

Work & Career
일과 직업

001 It's now or never.
002 I can feel it in my bones.
003 You've got what they want.
004 This project is my baby.
005 I'm flat broke.
006 Been there, done that.
007 I'm in over my head.
008 It's a foot in the door.
009 I'm not sweating it.
010 YOLO(You Only Live Once)
011 It was a close call.
012 Working around the clock is a must to get ahead.
013 I owe you a big one.
014 I smell a rat.

It's now or never. 지금 아니면 안돼.

동분서주

I'm taking the afternoon off.
오늘 오후에 조퇴할 거야.

Kell2013

What's wrong?
무슨 일 있어?

동분서주

🎵 grad school: 대학원

I have a grad school interview.
대학원 인터뷰가 있어.

Kell2013

What? You haven't told me anything about this.
뭐? 그런 말 한 적 없잖아.

동분서주

🎵 chew ~ over: ~에 대해 곰곰이 생각하다

I've been chewing this issue over since I don't know when.
이 문제에 대해 오랫동안 고민해왔어.

Kell2013

...

동분서주

♪have a feeling ~: ~한 예감이 들어, ~한 것 같아

I have a feeling this is a dead-end job for me.
나한텐 여기가 가망 없는 직장이라는 예감이 들어.

 Kell2013

I see. But you said you liked working there...
그렇구나. 그래도 너 거기서 일하는 거 좋아했잖아…

 동분서주

I do. But time waits for no one.
그랬지. 하지만 모든 일에는 때가 있어.

 Kell2013

But still...
그래도…

 동분서주

It's now or never.
지금 아니면 안돼.

 Kell2013

Well, good luck then.
그럼 행운을 빌게.

More to Talk!

 지지, 응원과 관련된 표현

Which team are you rooting for? 어느 팀을 응원하니?
Hope all goes well. 다 잘 되길 바란다.
I'll always be there for you. 항상 네 곁에 있을게.
She has a supportive family. 그녀는 지원해주는 가족이 있어.
He became financially independent right after graduation. 그는 졸업 직후 경제적으로 자립했어.

CHAT 01 **15**

I can feel it in my bones!

감이 와!

빈

I need a favor. Can I borrow your blue blazer?
부탁이 있어. 니 파란색 재킷 좀 빌려줄래?

Of course. You have good timing! Just picked it up from the cleaner's. lol
당연하지. 타이밍 좋네! 방금 세탁소에서 찾아왔거든 ㅋㅋㅋ

빈

Awesome! Thank you!!! I'll stop by tonight to pick it up.
짱인데! 고마워!!! 낼 가지러 갈게.

Cool. What's the occasion?
좋아. 무슨 특별한 일 있어?

빈

I've got an interview. They're looking for a new assistant manager at work.
인터뷰가 있어. 회사에서 새로 대리 될 사람을 뽑고 있거든.

I'm sure you'll get it. You are the star employee after all. ;)
넌 분명 해낼 거야. 누가 뭐래도 넌 스타 직원이잖아…

빈

Oh, I'm going to get it. I can feel it in my bones.
응. 해낼 거야. 감이 와!

Confident much?
자신감 충만?

빈

You know it! I've been there only two years and have been employee of the month like 9 times already.
알잖아! 나 겨우 2년차인데 모범직원으로 벌써 아홉 차례나 뽑혔어.

백조
lol
ㅋㅋㅋ

빈

Not only that but I know the hiring manager. She's super nice and told me to apply for the position herself.
게다가 인사과 부장님도 알고. 무지 친절하시고 나한테 지원하라고 말해준 것도 그분이야.

🔖 **Not that you'll need it.**: (간절히 바라지 않아도 이미 다 된 일이라고 확신하며) 그럴 필요 없겠지만.

백조
Nice. Well, good luck. Not that you'll need it.
잘됐네. 행운을 빌어. 뭐 행운씩이나 필요하지도 않겠지만.

빈

🔖 **Thx**: Thanks의 인터넷 약자

Haha thx. Gotta go though. I'll give you a call tonight when I get out of work.
고마워. 근데 가야겠다. 일 끝나고 오늘 밤에 전화할게.

🔖 **K**: OK의 인터넷 약자

백조
K. See you later.
오케. 나중에 봐.

More to Talk!

 자신감에 관한 표현

Don't worry, I've got this! 걱정 마. 알아서 할게.
Piece of cake! 누워서 떡 먹기지!
I am in total control of the situation. 상황은 완전히 내 손 안에 있어.
I have no doubt in my mind. 추호의 의심도 없어.
I'm a perfect fit! 내가 딱이야!

CHAT 01 **17**

You've got what they want.
넌 그들이 원하는 걸 가졌어.

Kell2013
> Coffee tomorrow?
> 낼 커피 어때?

♪ go on a biz trip: 출장 가다 / biz: business의 약어   **Jas**
> Sorry. I'm going on a biz trip.
> 미안. 출장 가게 됐어.

Kell2013
> Again? Where to?
> 또? 어디로?

Jas
> Singapore.
> 싱가포르.

Kell2013 ♪ most of the time: 대부분, 거의 모든 시간 동안
> It seems like you're out of the country most of time.
> 넌 거의 맨날 해외에 있는 거 같더라.

♪ attract investors: 투자자를 영입하다   **Jas**
> I need to attract more foreign investors.
> 더 많은 해외 투자가들을 끌어들여야 하거든.

18 SNS 잉글리시 톡

Kell2013

🎵 Don't worry about a thing: 걱정할 거 하나도 없어, 걱정하지 마

Don't worry about a thing. They'll definitely want to invest.
하나도 걱정할 거 없어. 그 사람들은 분명히 투자하고 싶어할 거야.

🎵 Thanx: Thanks의 약어   Jas

Thanx.
고마워.

 Kell2013   🎵 You've got what they want: 넌 그들이 원하는 걸 갖고 있어, 네가 적임자야.

I'm telling you. You've got what they want.
정말이야. 넌 그 사람들이 원하는 걸 가졌잖아.

🎵 pep talk: 격려의 말   Jas

Thanks for the pep talk. :)
격려 고마워.

 Kell2013   🎵 Anytime/any time: 언제든, (그런 걸로) 뭘.

Anytime. :D
뭐 그쯤이야. :D

🎵 You just made my day: 너 때문에 행복해졌다. 너 때문에 기분이 좋아졌다   Jas

No, really. You just made my day! :)
아니, 정말이야. 너 땜에 기분 좋아졌어.

 More to Talk!

 격려, 위로와 관련된 표현

Thank you for your encouragement. 격려해줘서 고마워.
I was moved by his honest words. 그의 정직한 말에 감동 받았어.
I feel much better after seeing you. 널 만나니까 훨씬 기운이 나.
Tell me something comforting. 뭔가 위로의 말 좀 해줘.
Don't try to sweet-talk me. 사탕발림하려 하지 마.
I'm flattered. 과찬이네.

ChitChat 004

This project is my baby.
이 프로젝트는 내 분신이야.

 천사표

🎵 work from paycheck to paycheck: 그날 벌어 그날 먹고 산다, 먹고 살기 바쁘게 산다

How's freelancing these days?
Still working paycheck to paycheck?
요즘 프리랜스 일 어때? 여전히 그날 벌어 그날 먹고 사는 중이야?

🎵 at the moment: 바로 지금, 이순간   Kell2013

Things are going great. Got a couple projects at the moment.
잘 풀리고 있어. 지금 두세 가지 프로젝트를 맡았거든.

 천사표

Good to hear!
잘됐네!

🎵 n: and의 약어   Kell2013

Yeah n they all pay pretty well... except one.
응. 급구 보수도 꽤 괜찮아… 한 가지만 빼고.

 천사표   🎵 take on: 떠맡다

So why even take it on? Time is money and
you can't afford to waste yours!
그런 걸 뭐하러 맡아? 시간이 돈인데 낭비할 여유 없잖아!

🎵 potential: 가능성   Kell2013

This is different. It doesn't pay much but it's got potential.
이건 달라. 돈은 별로 안되지만 가능성이 있거든.

 천사표

Oh? Do tell.
오? 얘기 좀 해봐.

🎵All I can say is...: 지금 당장은 …만 말할 수 있다   Kell2013

All I can say is that it's super exciting.
지금으로선 이 일이 넘 재밌다는 말밖에 할 수 없어.

 천사표   🎵tease: 놀리다. 애태우다

...you're just going to tease me like that?
…그렇게 감질나게 할 거야?

🎵blow you away: 너를 완전히 감동시킬 거야   Kell2013

Sorry. I signed a confidentiality agreement. :/ But in a few months you'll find out. It's going to blow you away!
미안. 내가 비밀 계약에 싸인했거든. 몇 달 지남 알게 될 거야. 완전 깜짝 놀랄걸!

 천사표

Wow! You sound really enthusiastic.
와우! 너 제대로 뻘받은 거 같은데.

🎵baby: 애지중지하는 것, 분신   Kell2013

Yeah! This project is my baby. I'm so excited!!!
응! 이 프로젝트는 내 분신이거든. 완전 신나!!!

More to Talk!

 급여에 관한 표현

The minimum wage in this city isn't high enough. 이 도시의 최저 임금은 그리 높지 않다.

The salary is lower at C Company but they don't require as much overtime. 급여는 C사가 더 낮지만 거기서는 시간외 근무를 많이 요구하지 않는다.

They give raises every year after doing a performance review. 인사고과를 실시한 후 매년 봉급인상을 해준다.

The salespeople at that store are a little pushy because they make commission off what they sell. 그 상점의 판매원들은 자신이 판매한 것에 대해 수수료를 받기 때문에 약간 저돌적이다.

After taxes and living expenses there isn't much money left for savings. 세금과 생활비를 내고 나면 저축할 돈이 별로 없다.

ChitChat 005

I'm flat broke.
나 완전 거덜났어.

Tae

Are you still playing that game?
아직도 그 게임 하고 있냐?

🎵 raid: 급습, 기습 / sword: 검, 칼

겜폐남

Yeah, I just need to finish this raid and get my epic sword
응. 그냥 이 레이드를 끝내고 에픽 스워드만 찾으면 돼.

Tae

Why don't you log off and join me for a drink?
게임 그만하고 한잔 하러 나가자.

🎵 flat broke: 무일푼의, 완전 파산한

겜폐남

I can't. I'm flat broke.
안돼. 한 푼도 없어.

Tae 🎵 get off your ass: (엉덩이 들고) 일어나다(친한 친구 사이에 쓸 수 있는 표현)

Maybe you'd have more money if you got off your ass and found a job.
너 당장 일어나서 직장 구하면 돈을 더 벌지 않을까.

bux: bucks의 약어, 달러   겜폐남

I AM working! This sword is worth 500 bux!
나 일하는 중이거든! 이 검은 500달러나 돼!

 Tae IRL: in real life의 인터넷 약자, 실제로

IRL?
실제로?

leave me alone: 나 좀 가만 둬, 방해하지 마   겜폐남

Yeah, so leave me alone while I work!
그래, 그러니까 근무중일 땐 방해하지 마!

 Tae looks like ~: (It) looks like를 줄인 표현, ~할 것 같다. / Drinks are on you. 술은 네가 사.

Looks like drinks are on you next time!
담엔 네가 술 한턱 낼 모양이네!

More to Talk!

 방해와 관련된 표현

Am I disturbing you? 나 때문에 방해되니?

Don't disturb me. I have loads of work to do. 방해하지 마. 할 일이 산더미야.

I didn't mean to stand in the(your) way. 네 앞길을 가로막을 의도는 없었어.

Don't let the weather get you down. 날씨 때문에 기분 꿀꿀해지지 마.

I'm on a diet. Hunger is distracting me from doing work. 다이어트 중야. 허기 때문에 일에 집중이 잘 안돼.

Been there, done that.
다 겪어봤어.

백조
🔖 u: you의 인터넷 약자

U know what I just did?
나 방금 뭐 했게?

동분서주
What?
뭐?

백조
🔖 post: 게재하다, 게시하다

Posted my resume.
이력서 올렸어.

동분서주
Oh really?
아, 그래?

백조
It's soooo stressful!
너~~~무 스트레스야!

🔖 Been there, done that: I have been there and done that.
나도 그랬던 적이 있었다. 다 겪어 봤다, 새로울 것이 딱히 없다.

동분서주
Been there, done that.
나도 다 겪어봤지.

백조
I'm so stressed out.
정말 스트레스 받아.

♪odds: 확률, 가능성 동분서주

What are the odds?
가능성은?

백조  ♪slim: 희박한, 가냘픈 / fierce: 사나운, 치열한

Slim. Competition is fierce.
희박해. 경쟁이 치열하거든.

♪hands-on experience: 현장 경험 동분서주

But you've got loads of hands-on experience...
그래도 넌 현장 경험이 엄청 많잖아…

백조  ♪be tired of ~: ~하기 싫증난, 지겨운 / working part-time: 시간제 근무하기

Maybe too much. I'm tired of working part-time.
너무 많아서 탈이지. 시간제 근무는 이제 지긋지긋해.

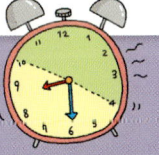

♪make it: 해내다, 성공하다 동분시주

Hope you make it this time!
이번엔 꼭 됐음 좋겠다!

More to Talk!

 경험과 관련된 표현

Have you ever met anyone you met on-line in person? 온라인에서 만난 사람을 직접 만난 적 있어?

It was my first time on a blind date. 소개팅에 나간 건 그게 처음이었어.

Now I've seen it all. 별 꼴 다 보겠네.

Money has never made man happy. 돈이 사람을 행복하게 해준 적은 없다.(벤저민 프랭클린의 명언)

Don't let this happen again! 다신 이런 일 없게 해!

ChitChat 007

I'm in over my head.
난 도저히 감당 안돼.

Jas

🎵 bout: about의 약어

> Things are finally slowing down at work! How bout you?
> 이제야 일이 좀 천천히 돌아가네! 넌 어때?

동분서주

> Lucky you. I barely have enough time to shower in the mornings...
> 좋겠수. 난 아침마다 샤워도 간신히 하는데...

Jas

🎵 junior staff: 부하 직원

> I see they work their junior staff pretty hard!
> 부하 직원을 아주 제대로 굴리나 보네!

🎵 I'll say: 그럼, 정말 그래

동분서주

> I'll say! And they want me to take all these foreign language tests...
> 그렇다니깨! 거기다 온갖 외국어 시험들을 보라질 않나...

Jas

> Huh? I thought once you got the job you wouldn't have to worry about that kind of stuff.
> 그래? 일단 취업한 다음에는 그런 거 걱정할 일 없을 줄 알았는데.

🎵 check one's specs: 스펙을 확인하다 / specs: specifications의 약어   동분서주

> So did I. Times sure have changed. Even after being hired they constantly check your specs.
> 나두. 시대가 변하긴 했나 봐. 취업된 후에도 계속 스펙을 체크하니까.

Jas

So it seems... How are you coping?
그런 거 같네... 넌 어떻게, 견딜 만해?

be good at ~: ~를 잘한다. / keep up with ~: ~를 따라잡다, 발을 맞추다   동분서주

Not well. Everyone here is really good at English, Chinese, and even Japanese! I can't keep up with them. I'm in over my head. :'(
별로. 여기서는 다들 영어, 중국어, 하물며 일본어까지 진짜 잘해! 따라갈 수가 없어. 완전 무리야. :'(

 Jas   take classes: 수강하다, 수업을 듣다

I started taking Chinese classes on the weekends. Any interest in joining?
나 주말마다 중국어 수업 듣기 시작했는데. 같이 해볼 맘 없어?

동분서주

Lots... but I work weekends too.
많지... 근데 난 주말에도 일해야 해.

스펙에 관한 표현

I'm thinking of volunteering abroad so I can beef up my resume.
해외 봉사해서 이력서 좀 보강해볼까 해.

A minimum TOEIC test score of 700 is required in order to be considered for employment. 취업하려면 최소한 700점의 토익점수가 필요하다.

His test scores are really high but in reality he is quite poor at English conversation. 그는 시험 점수는 굉장히 높은데 사실 영어회화는 잘 못한다.

Academics are important but you also have to have a decent amount of experience in the field. 학업도 중요하지만 적절한 현장 경험 역시 중요하다.

They are interested in people who are constantly trying to better themselves through study and volunteering. 그들은 학업과 봉사활동을 통해 끝없이 자신을 발전시키려는 사람들에게 호감을 가지고 있다.

 008

It's a foot in the door.
그 분야에 한 발 들여놓은 거야.

 백조

I heard the news about your interview with S Company! Congratulations!!!
S사하고 면접 본단 소식 들었어. 축하해!!!

💡 It's not that big a deal.: 그거 별 거 아냐.

King_Michael

Oh. It's not that big a deal...
아. 그게 뭐 대수라고.

 백조

Not that big a deal? This is huge! It's so hard to pass their initial tests!
별 거 아니라고? 대단한 거지! 1차 시험 통과가 얼마나 어려운데.

King_Michael

Yes, but it's still only an interview.
응. 그래도 그냥 면접일 뿐이야.

 백조

It's a foot in the door.
그건 그 분야에 한 발을 들여놓은 거야.

King_Michael

Yeah... I guess.
어... 그렇겠지.

 백조

You don't sound very excited.
어째 시큰둥하게 들린다?

King_Michael

It's just a lot of pressure. Plus my exams are coming. I'll be happy when all this is over with.
강 부담감 땜에 그래. 게다가 시험도 곧 있고. 이 모든 게 끝나야 살 만할 것 같아.

백조

🎤 I'll tell you what.: 있잖아, 실은 말이야.

Everything will be fine. I'll tell you what—if you pass the interview, I'll buy you dinner.
잘될 거야. 있지. 면접 통과하면 내가 저녁 살게.

King_Michael

Just dinner?
저녁만?

백조

Drinks too!
술도!

King_Michael

Sounds good to me. I'm going to go prepare for it now then.
좋아. 그럼 이제 준비하러 가야겠다.

백조

Good luck!
행운을 빈다!

More to Talk!

구직에 관한 표현

I've been to every recruiting agency in town; there just isn't any work out there! 여기 도시에 있는 리크루팅 에이전시란 에이전시는 다 가봤는데, 일자리가 아무데도 없는 거야!

There are several stages of interviews. 면접에는 몇 단계가 있어.

They get thousands of applicants everyday but hire very few. 지원자는 매일 수천 명씩 받는데 극소수만 뽑아.

I'm still waiting for a callback after my interview last month. 지난 달에 면접 보고 나서 아직 회신 기다리고 있어.

I'm not sweating it.
그쯤이야.

백조
Sorry to hear you didn't get the job. I know you really wanted it.
그 자리 안됐다며. 유감이다. 네가 정말 되고 싶었던 거 아는데.

🎵I'm not sweating it.: 별 거 아냐, 그쯤이야. **빈**
I'm not sweating it.
뭐 별 거 아냐.

백조
What? You said you'd die if you didn't get the job.
뭐? 그 자리 안되면 죽고 만다며.

🎵opportunities: 기회 **빈**
Yeah, well... there will be more opportunities.
응, 뭐, 기회 더 있으니까.

백조
🎵optimistic: 낙관적인
That's pretty optimistic of you.
꽤 낙관적인데.

Yeah. I'm feeling pretty positive. And I just saw the person they picked.
응. 긍정적으로 생각하려고. 글구 누가 뽑혔는지 방금 봤거든.

And?
그래서?

🎵 prob: problem, 문제

He's sooooooooo hot.
그 사람 지이~~~인짜 멋있어.

🎵 rofl: rolling on the floor, 빵터짐, 너무 우스워서 바닥을 구르며 웃음

rofl NOW I get it.
빵터진다. 이제 알갓쓰.

More to Talk!

낙관성과 관련된 표현

You seem quite positive despite the circumstances. 너 그런 상황에도 꽤 긍정적인 거 같구나.

If the glass is half full, you are an optimist. 잔이 절반은 차 있다(고 생각하)면 넌 낙관주의자야.

If the glass is half empty, you are a pessimist. 잔이 절반은 비었다(고 생각하)면 넌 비관주의자야.

I always try to look on the bright side of things. 난 늘 사물을 낙관적으로 보려고 애를 써.

When life gives you lemons, make lemonade. 삶이 너에게 레몬을 주면, 레모네이드를 만들어라.

ChitChat 010

YOLO (You Only Live Once)
인생 두 번 사냐.

빈

> My colleague just got back to me about that internship we were talking about.
> 전에 너랑 얘기했던 인턴십 관해서 동료가 방금 답신해줬어.

백조

> Sweet! What did he say?
> 잘됐네! 뭐래?

빈

> They are still looking for someone, but unfortunately it's unpaid.
> 아직 사람을 구하고 있긴 한데, 무급이래.

백조

> Oh... that's cool I guess.
> 아... 괜찮을 거 같은데.

빈

> They at least pay for lunch and transportation costs. You should do it just to get your foot in the door.
> 적어도 점심이랑 교통비는 준대. 그 분야에 발을 들여놓으려면 해야지.

백조

> Do they usually hire their interns?
> 보통 인턴을 고용한대?

빈

🎤 networking opportunities: 인맥 쌓을 기회(들)

> Only about 50%. But there are also lots of networking opportunities.
> 50퍼센트 정도만. 근데 인맥을 쌓을 기회도 많대.

🔎 **YOLO:** (=You only live once)인생은 한 번뿐이다, 두 번 사는 사람 없다.

> Hmm... okay! Why not? YOLO, right? lol
> 흠… 좋아! 안될 거 있나? YOLO, 그치? ㅋㅋㅋ

> Huh? What is YOLO?
> 엉? YOLO가 뭔데?

> You don't know YOLO?
> hahahaha It means you only live once!
> 몰라? 하하하하. "인생 두 번 사냐"란 말야!

> Ahhh yeah I think I've heard that before.
> 아~ 응. 들어본 거 같다.

🔎 **I bet ~:** ~를 장담하다 / **cray:** crazy의 채팅 속어

> I bet you don't know what cray is either.
> 넌 분명히 cray도 모르겠구나.

> No idea. All I know is that you'd better not talk like that in the interview. lol
> 몰라. 분명한 건 너 면접 때 그런 식으로 말하지 않는 게 좋겠단 것뿐 ㅋㅋㅋ

More to Talk!

 인생과 관련된 표현

Life's too short to sweat small stuff. 사소한 것에 신경쓰기엔 삶은 너무 짧다.
Life's short; eat dessert first. 인생은 짧다. 그러니 디저트를 먼저 먹어라.
You only get one life so make the most of it. 인생은 한 번뿐이니 최대한 이용해라.
Carpe diem! (Seize the day!) 현재를 즐겨라!

It was a close call. 십년감수했어.

Kell2013
Didn't sleep a wink last night.
어젯밤 한숨도 못 잤어.

천사표
Why not?
왜?

Kell2013 🔖 meet a deadline: 마감 날짜(시간)를 맞추다
I had a deadline to meet.
마감 지키느라고.

천사표
Did you make it on time?
제때 마쳤어?

Kell2013
Of course.
당근.

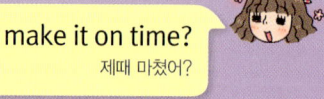
Kell2013 🔖 ruin one's reputation: 평판이 나빠지다
Breaking deadlines would ruin my reputation as a freelancer.
마감을 어겼다간 프리랜서로서 평판 끝이야.

천사표
I agree.
맞아.

Kell2013 🔖 It was a close call: 아슬아슬했다, 십년감수했다
Well, it was a close call.
십년감수했지 뭐야.

🎵 catch up on some sleep: 밀린 잠을 보충하다

Go home and catch up on some sleep.
집에 가서 밀린 잠 좀 자.

Kell2013

I will. Thx.
응. 고마워.

🎵 be about to ~: ~하던 참이다, 막 ~하려 하다

Actually, now you're about to harm your reputation.
실은 지금 네 평판이 나빠지려는 참이야.

Kell2013

???

Don't you remember?
기억 안나?

We were supposed to meet 1 hour ago!!!
우리 한 시간 전에 만나기로 했잖아!!!

Kell2013

🎵 stick around: 그 자리에 그대로 있다, 딴 데 가지 않다.

Ugh... Stick around. I'm on my way.
억... 거기 있어. 금방 갈게.

 기다림과 관계된 표현

Stay where you are. I'll be there in a bit. 거기서 기다려. 금방 갈게.
Stay put. I'm coming! 꼼짝 말고 있어. 곧 간다!
Don't go anywhere. I'll be there in 10. 아무데도 가지 마. 10분 정도면 도착할 거야.
Wait a sec. I'll be right with you. 1초만. 금방 갈게.
I'll be right over. I'm already there. 금방 간다. 다 왔어.

Working around the clock is a must to get ahead.
성공하려면 24시간 내내 일해야 해.

동분서주

Are you working late again?
또 늦게까지 일해?

Kell2013

Yeah, I have a deadline tomorrow afternoon.
응. 마감이 내일 오후야.

동분서주

🔖 **be burn out**: 기력이 완전 소진되다, 지쳐 쓰러지다

Well, don't work too hard. You might burn yourself out!
쉬엄쉬엄 해. 그러다 쓰러질라.

🔖 **work around the clock**: 24시간 일하다 / **a must to get ahead**: 성공의 필수 조건   Kell2013

They say that working around the clock is a must to get ahead.
성공하려면 24시간 내내 일해야 한다고 하잖아.

동분서주

Well, don't forget me when you get too far ahead!
그럼, 너~무 성공한 다음에 나 잊지 마.

🎵 BFF: best friend forever 절친

Kell2013

Lol. How can I forget my BF?!?
ㅋㅋㅋ 내 절친을 어떻게 잊겠니?

 동분서주 🎵 little people: 돈 없고 힘없는 사람들

Just don't forget the little people!
돈 없는 사람들 잊지 말라고!

Kell2013

lol I'll buy you lunch every day!
ㅋㅋㅋ 맨날 점심 사줄게.

동분서주 🎵 You better. =You'd better: 그러는 게 좋을걸, 그래야지.

You better. ;)
고래야줘 ;)

 More to Talk!

 과로에 관한 표현

Working too hard is bad for your health. 과로하면 건강에 해로워.

All work and no play makes you a boring person! 일만 하고 놀 줄 모르면 재미없는 사람 된다!

The deadline's been extended so don't overwork yourself. 마감날이 연기됐으니 과로하지 마.

Her boss worked himself to death. 그녀의 사장이 과로로 사망했어.

ChitChat 013

I owe you a big one.
크게 신세졌다.

 겜폐남
> I heard you have a friend who owns a game company.
> 너 게임 회사 운영하는 친구 있댔지.

Tae
> Yeah, Jas. He's a pretty cool guy. What's up?
> 응, Jas라고. 꽤 괜찮은 친구야. 왜?

 겜폐남
> Do you know if he's hiring?
> 혹시 사람 뽑는지 알아?

Tae
> Not sure, but I can ask him. Why?
> 잘 모르지만 물어볼 순 있어. 왜?

 겜폐남
> You know how much I love to play games, and I thought it would be fun to work at a game company.
> 나 게임 엄청 좋아하는 거 알잖아. 게임회사에서 일하면 재밌을 거 같아서.

under stress: 스트레스 받는

Tae
> Yeah, but I don't think it's all fun and games. Jas always seems to be under stress.
> 응, 근데 늘 재밌고 게임만 하는 건 아닐 텐데. Jas는 늘 스트레스 받는 것 같더라.

겜폐남

You know what they say?
Nothing in life is easy.
그런 말 못 들어봤어? 인생에 쉬운 일은 없다고.

🎵 ain't: 비표준어, be동사 + not의 축약형   Tae

Ain't that the truth.
암. 만고의 진리지.

 겜폐남

Do you think you can introduce me to Jas and maybe get me an interview?
나 좀 Jas한테 소개시켜줘서 면접 좀 보게 해줄 수 있어?

Tae

Sure, I'm supposed to have lunch with him this week.
I'll introduce you two.
고럼. 이번 주에 점심 먹기로 했거든. 소개해줄게.

 겜폐남

🎵 owe someone a big one: ~에게 큰 신세를 지다

Thanks, I owe you a big one.
고마워. 신세 크게 졌다.

More to Talk!

 스트레스에 관련된 표현

Too much stress can cause a sleep disorder. 스트레스가 과하면 수면장애가 생길 수 있다.
I wanna know how to de-stress. 스트레스 해소하는 법을 알고 싶어.
How can I get rid of my stress? 어떻게 하면 스트레스를 없앨 수 있니?
I just wanna work in a less stressful work environment. 난 그냥 스트레스 덜 받는 작업 환경에서 일하고 싶어.
Chronic stress affects your immune system. 만성적 스트레스는 면역체계에 영향을 준다.

ChitChat 014

I smell a rat.
끰새가 수상한데.

빈
🖊 let ~ go: ~를 보내다, 가게 하다, 해고하다
> They let another person go today.
> 회사에서 오늘 한 명 더 해고했어.

🖊 severe: 가혹한, 심한 **천사표**
> You've got to be kidding me! Your new manager is so severe!
> 설마 그럴 수가! 너네 신임 점장 넘 심하다!

빈
🖊 You're telling me.: 내 말이 그거라니까.
> You're telling me! He fired this one for not being "cheery" enough.
> 내 말이! 그 사람을 해고시킨 건 충분히 "명랑하지" 않아서 그랬대.

천사표
> Dang.
> 망할.

빈
🖊 ppl: people의 약자, 사람들
> Yeah. And this person is one of cheeriest ppl I know. Something is not right.
> 응 거기다. 그 사람은 내가 아는 한 젤 명랑한 사람이야. 뭔가 이상해.

천사표
> You think there is something else going on?
> 뭔가 다른 꿍꿍이가 있는 거 같니?

빈

Well I heard that he used to manage another café in town that went out of business.
음, 그 사람이 전에 시내에 다른 카페를 운영했는데, 그게 파산했대.

 천사표

Oh?
오?

 빈

Apparently he was really close with the staff there. Like family.
그 사람은 거기 직원들하고 정말 가까웠대. 가족처럼.

 천사표

Uh-huh...
어~ 오우…

 빈

Well most of them are still looking for jobs... And our place just lost a bunch of staff!
그 사람들 대부분이 아직 일자릴 찾고 있는데… 우리 카페는 방금 직원을 잔뜩 해고했고!

  천사표

I smell a rat!
뭔가 낌새가 수상해.

More to Talk!

 의심과 관련된 표현

Something fishy is going on at the office. 회사에 뭔가 꿍꿍이가 있다.
A lot of strange things have been going on. 많은 이상한 일들이 일어나고 있다.
Does he seem suspicious to you? 그 남자 좀 수상하지 않니?
I wouldn't tell her; I'm not sure she is trustworthy. 나라면 그 여자한테 말 안할 거야. 그 여자 믿을 만한지 잘 모르겠어.

Review — Words & Expressions — CHAT 01

ChitChat 001 — p 14
It's now or never.

take the afternoon of 오전 근무만 하다, 조퇴하다
grad school 대학원
chew over ~ ~에 대해 곰곰이 생각하다
since I don't know when 까마득하게 옛날부터
have a feeling ~ ~한 느낌이 들다
dead-end job 가망 없는 직업
Time waits for no one. 모든 일에는 때가 있다.
It's now or never. 지금 아니면 안돼.
root 응원하다
supportive 지원해주는, 지지하는
financially independent 경제적으로 독립한

ChitChat 002 — p 16
I can feel it in my bones.

I need a favor. 부탁할 게 있어.
the cleaner's 세탁소
stop by 들르다
What's the occasion? 무슨 특별한 일 있어?
assistant manager 대리
I can feel it in my bones. 감이 와.
You know it! 알잖아!
employee of the month 이달의 모범 사원
hiring manager 인사과 부장
Not that you'll need it. 그럴 필요가 있단 건 아니고.
get out of work 퇴근하다
piece of cake 식은 죽 먹기, 누워서 떡 먹기
have no doubt 의심할 여지가 없다

I'm a perfect fit. 난 딱이야, 내가 적임자야.

ChitChat 003 — p 18
You've got what they want.

go on a biz trip 출장 가다
most of time 대개
attract investors 투자가를 영입하다
Don't worry about a thing. 걱정할 거 하나도 없어.
invest 투자하다
You've got what they want. 넌 그들이 원하는 것을 가졌어.
pep talk 격려의 말
You made my day. 너 때문에 오늘 기분 좋아졌어.
encouragement 격려
move 감동하다
comforting 위로가 되는
sweet-talk someone ~에게 사탕발림하다
I'm flattered. 과찬이야.

ChitChat 004 — p 20
This project is my baby.

freelancing 프리랜스 일
work paycheck to paycheck 하루 벌어 하루 먹고살다
Things are going great. 잘 풀리고 있어.
take on 떠맡다
afford ~할 여유가 있다
potential 가능성
All I can say is… (지금) 말할 수 있는 것은…
tease 놀리다

CHAT 01

confidentiality agreement 비밀 계약
in a few months 몇 달 있으면
This project is my baby. 이 프로젝트는 나의 분신이야.
overtime 시간 외 근무
performance review 인사 고과
commission 수수료

ChitChat 005   p 22
I'm flat broke.

Join me for a drink. 나랑 술 한잔 하러 가자.
I'm flat broke. 나 완전 거덜났어.
bux: bucks, 달러
in real life 실제로
Leave me alone. 나 좀 내버려둬.
Drinks are on me. 술값은 내가 낸다.

ChitChat 006   p 24
Been there, done that.

post one's resume ~의 이력서를 게재하다
Been there, done that. 다 겪어봤어.
stressed out 완전히 스트레스 받는
fierce 치열한
hands-on experience 현장 경험
work part-time 시간제 근무하다
make it 성공하다, 이뤄내다
I've seen it all. 별 꼴 다 보겠네.

ChitChat 007   p 26
I'm in over my head.

slow down 속도가 줄다
Lucky you. 잘됐네, 좋겠네.
junior staff 부하 직원
I'll say. 정말 그래.
that kind of stuff 그런 거
I'm in over my head. 도저히 감당이 안돼.
take classes 수강하다

ChitChat 008   p 28
It's a foot in the door.

congratulation 축하
Congratulations. 축하해.
It's not that big a deal. 그거 별 거 아냐.
initial: 초기의
It's a foot in the door. 그 분야에 첫발을 디딘 거야.
pressure 압박감
I'll tell you what. 있잖아, 실은 말이야.
pass the interview 면접에 합격하다
preliminary 예비의
applicant 지원자
callback 회신

ChitChat 009   p 30
I'm not sweating it.

I'm not sweating it. 그쯤이야, 별 거 아냐.
optimistic 낙관적인
positive 긍정적인

CHAT 01

circumstances 상황
optimist 낙관론자
pessimist 비관론자
look on the bright side 낙관적으로 생각하다

ChitChat 010   p 32
YOLO (You Only Live Once)

colleague 회사 동료
transportation cost 교통비
hire 고용하다
networking 인맥 쌓기
YOLO(You Only Live Once) 인생 두 번 사냐
sweat 신경 쓰다
make the most of 최대한 이용하다
Carpe diem! 현재를 즐겨라, 순간을 즐겨라.

ChitChat 011   p 34
It was a close call.

do (not) sleep a wink 한숨도 못 자다
on time 제때에
break deadlines 마감을 어기다
ruin one's reputation 평판이 나빠지다
reputation 평판
freelancer 프리랜서
It was a close call 십년감수했어.
catch up on some sleep 밀린 잠을 자다
harm one's reputation 평판에 금 가다
stick around 거기 (머물러) 있다

ChitChat 012   p 36
Working around the clock is a must to get ahead.

burn oneself out 지쳐 쓰러지다
Working around the clock is a must to get ahead. 성공하려면 24시간 내내 일해야 해.
BF best friend, 절친
little people 돈 없고 힘없는 사람들
You better. 그래야지, 그러는 게 좋을걸.
overwork 과로하다
work to death 과로사하다

ChitChat 013   p 38
I owe you a big one.

own 소유하다
under stress 스트레스 받은
I owe you a big one. 너한테 크게 신세졌어.
sleep disorder 수면 장애
immune system 면역체계

ChitChat 014   p 40
I smell a rat.

let someone go ~를 해고하다
severe 가혹한, 심한
go out of business 파산하다
staff 직원
I smell a rat. 낌새가 수상해.
fishy 수상한
suspicious 수상한

CHAT 02

Appearance
외모

- 015 You should call ahead for an appointment.
- 016 How about bangs?
- 017 I went a little too far…
- 018 I couldn't even recognize her!
- 019 I can't get rid of this backne.
- 020 You've got to look the part.
- 021 I have NOTHING to wear.
- 022 You look fresh off the runway.
- 023 Isn't it too showy for the first date?
- 024 I look like I just rolled out of bed.
- 025 What's your point?

ChitChat 015

You should call ahead for an appointment.
예약하려면 미리 전화해야 해.

 동분서주
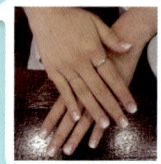

 동분서주
See this?
이거 보여?

백조
Nice! Newly done?
예쁘다! 새로 받은 거야?

 동분서주
♪ squeeze ~ in: (틈 사이로) 끼워 넣다
Yup! They squeezed me in at the last minute.
응! 막판에 날 넣어줬어.

They look flawless. I love it.
완벽한 거 같다. 맘에 들어.

 동분서주
♪ affordable: 알맞은, 저렴한
They do a fantastic job while keeping it affordable.
엄청 잘하는데 가격도 착해.

Maybe I should visit the place. Where is it again?
거기 가봐야겠다. 어디랬지?

 동분서주
♪ fl: floor의 약어 / bldg.: 빌딩의 약어
On the 1st fl of my office bldg.
회사 건너편 건물 1층이야.

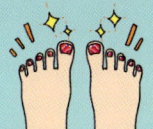
🎵 **while I'm at it:** ~한 김에, 내친 김에

백조

While I'm at it, I'll get a pedicure, too.
내친 김에 페디큐어도 받아야겠다.

동분서주

You should call ahead for an appointment.
먼저 예약 전화 해두는 게 좋을걸.

백조

I. C. Well, how often do you get a pedi?
알써. 근데 페디큐어는 얼마나 자주 받니?

동분서주

Maybe once or twice a month. I also do it myself.
한 달에 한두 번 정도. 내가 할 때도 있어.

백조

But removing dead skin is really a pain.
하지만 각질 제거는 넘 귀찮잖아.

동분서주

True.
마쟈.

백조

🎵 **after a while:** 한동안

Plus it makes your back hurt after a while.
게다가 통허리도 아쓰나니까.

동분서주

🎵 **plz:** please의 약자 / **w/u:** with you

Um, let me tag along w/u. Make it for two plz.
나도 갈게. 두 명으로 예약해줘.

More to Talk!

예약과 관계된 표현

I called to make a reservation. 예약을 위해 전화했습니다.

The shop takes walk-in customers too. 그 샵은 예약 없이 가는 손님도 받는다.

I called two days ahead to get an appointment. 예약을 위해 이틀 전에 전화했다.

They were fully booked so I couldn't get my nails done. 예약이 다 차서 네일 관리를 못 받았다.

Can I make a reservation for 2 at 5:00? 5시에 두 명 예약할 수 있나요?

ChitChat 016

How about bangs?
앞머리 자르는 게 어때?

Kell2013
Hey. Where r u?
안녕. 어디야?

천사표
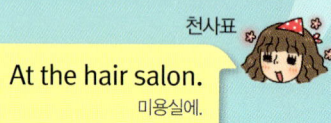
At the hair salon.
미용실에.

Kell2013
Getting a perm?
파마하는 거야?

천사표
Nope. I got that done last week. Remember?
아니. 지난 주에 했잖아. 기억해?

Kell2013
Whoops! Now I remember.
앗! 이제 기억났어.

♬ **pick on**: 괴롭히다, 집적거리다

천사표
My husband is picking on me about my new hairdo.):(
남편이 새로 한 머리 땜에 생트집이야.

Kell2013
Um, ur hair looked good in the pic.
사진에선 이쁘던데.

🔍 **do the magic:** 마법처럼 작용하다
Photo filter did the magic.;)
앱빨이었어.

Kell2013
Really?
진짜로?

Really really. So what should I do to look younger?
진짜진짜로. 나 어려 보이려면 어떻게 해야 할까?

Kell2013
How about bangs? It'll take 10 years off of you.
앞머리 자르는 게 어때? 10년은 어려 보일걸.

More to Talk!

 미용 관련 표현 1

I'd like to get my hair straightened. 스트레이트 파마 하고 싶어.

You need to trim your hair to keep it healthy. 건강한 머릿결을 유지하려면 머리를 다듬어야 해.

She had her long hair cut short after breaking up with her bf. 그녀는 남친과 헤어지고 나서 긴 머리를 짧게 잘랐어.

It's hard to grow out of a bad haircut. 머리를 잘못 자르면 도로 기르기가 힘들어.

Shampoo residue can cause an itchy scalp. 샴푸 잔여물 때문에 두피가 가려울 수 있어.

ChitChat 017

I went a little too far…
나 좀 오버했어…

 겜폐남
> Wanna grab a bite? I'm down the street from your place.
> 뭐 좀 먹을래? 너네 집 근처 길가에 있는데.

빈
> No. I'm never leaving this house again!
> 싫어. 다신 집 밖에 안 나갈 거야.

 겜폐남
> Lol why's that?
> ㅋㅋㅋ 왜 그런데?

🔊 It's a disaster.: 최악이다. 완전 망했다.

빈
> My hair. It's a disaster. I just got the worst haircut of my life.
> 내 머리. 완전 망했어. 내 인생 최악의 머리라고.

 겜폐남
> They cut it a little too short? I'm sure it's not that bad.
> 좀 너무 짧게 자른 거야? 그렇게 심하기야 하려고.

빈
> It's waaaay too short. And blonde. :X
> 너어어어~무 짧아. 글구 금발.

 겜폐남
> Blonde? You dyed it too?
> 금발? 염색도 했어?

🎵 **main character:** 주인공, 주연 / **copy one's style:** ~의 스타일을 따라하다   빈

I was watching some American movie and the main character was so cute so I tried to copy her style.
미국 영화 보다가 주연이 넘 예쁘길래 그 여자처럼 하려고 했지.

빈

I went a little too far...
좀 오버해 버렸어…

젬페남

🎵 **throw on ~:** ~을 대충 걸치다, ~에 의지하다

There's not a thing you could do to make yourself look bad. How about throwing on a hat and meeting me?
넌 어떻게 해도 흉해 보일 리가 없어. 모자로 대충 가리고 만나는 게 어때?

빈

You buying?
니가 살 거야?

젬페남

🎵 **You coming?:** Are you coming?을 줄인 표현

Yeah. You coming?
그럼. 올 거야?

 Sure, why not? XD
고럼, 왜 아냐?

빈

 미용 관련 표현 2

I asked them to cut it shoulder length but look how short it is! 어깨길이로 잘라달라고 했는데 이렇게 짧은 것 좀 봐!

I ask them for a shampoo too because I love the way they massage my scalp. 나는 두피 마사지 받는 게 너무 좋아서 샴푸도 해달라고 해.

I've been getting my hair permed for years. 난 몇 년째 파마를 하고 있어.

Buying hair dye and coloring your hair at home is so much cheaper.
염색약을 사서 집에서 염색을 하면 훨씬 싸게 들어.

They also do eyebrow waxing and tanning there. 거기서는 눈썹 왁스와 태닝도 해.

More to Talk!

CHAT 02 **51**

I couldn't even recognize her!
걔 알아보지도 못하겠더라!

백조

빈! Guess who I met today.
빈, 내가 오늘 누굴 봤게.

빈

Who?
누군데?

백조

Joohee from high school.
고등학교 때 친구인 주희야.

빈

I haven't seen her in years. How is she?
걔 못본 지 몇 년 됐네. 어떻게 지낸대?

백조

I couldn't even recognize her.
걔 알아보지도 못하겠더라.

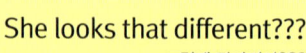
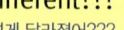

빈

She looks that different???
그렇게 달라졌어???

백조

🎵 lose weight: 살 빠지다

She lost soooo much weight.
She weighs half of what she did in HS.
살 너~무 뺀 거 있지. 고딩 때 대비 반쪽 됐어.

빈

Really?
구래?

 백조 🎵 on top of that: 그뿐 아니라, 게다가

On top of that, she underwent multiple plastic surgeries.
게다가 성형 수술도 잔뜩 했어.

🎵 speechless: 할 말 잃음, 헐   빈

I'm speechless. :-X
헐.

 백조 🎵 thing is: 문제는, 실은

Thing is...
문젠...

빈

???

 백조 🎵 full of oneself: 자만심이 가득 찬, 거만하게 구는

She seemed a little full of herself.
걔가 좀 거만해 보이더라.

빈

Oh, well...
뜨아...

미용 관련 표현 3

More to Talk!

She has had a lot of work done. 그녀는 성형 수술을 많이 했어.
I felt refreshed after getting a massage. 마사지를 받고 나니 개운해졌어.
Have you thought of getting a nose job? 너 코 수술할 생각 해봤니?
His aunt got facial Botox injections. 그의 숙모는 얼굴에 보톡스 주사를 맞았다.
I'm going to get permanent eyeliner done. 반영구 속눈썹 문신을 할 계획이야.

CHAT 02 **53**

ChitChat 019

I can't get rid of this backne.
내 등드름을 없앨 수가 없어.

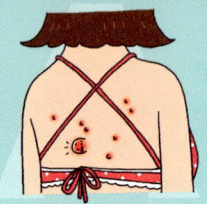

Kell2013

🎤 cuz of: because of의 약어

Why'd you cancel on the Busan trip? 백조 says it's cuz of work but I know that's not true.
부산 여행 왜 취소했니? 백조가 일 때문이라고 하던데 난 아닌 거 다 알아.

It's embarrassing.
민망해서 말하기 그래.

Kell2013 🎤 spill: 털어놔, 얘기해

I won't tell anyone. Spill.
아무한테도 말 안 할게. 빨랑 불어.

🎤 bathing suit: 수영복   동분서주

I don't want to wear a bathing suit.
수영복 입고 싶지 않아.

Kell2013

🎤 self-conscious: 자의식이 강한, 남의 시선을 의식하는

Oh, don't be silly. We all feel self-conscious about our bodies. But you're the skinniest one of us!
아, 바보같이. 우린 다들 몸에 대해 남의 시선을 의식하긴 해. 하지만 니가 우리 중에 젤로 말랐잖아!

Kell2013   🎤 bare: 헐벗다, 몸을 드러내다

If we can bare it all so can you!
우리도 괜찮은데 니가 왜 못해!

동분서주

It's not my weight. It's my skin.
몸무게 때문이 아냐. 피부가 문제야.

Kell2013

🔖 **immaculate:** 무결점의, 티없이 깔끔한

Your skin is immaculate!
니 피부는 완벽 그 자체야!

🔖 **backne:** back+ acne, 등과 여드름의 합성어, 등드름

동분서주

**Not my face... my body!
I can't get rid of this backne. :'(**
얼굴 말고… 몸! 내 등드름을 없앨 수가 없어!

Kell2013

🔖 **clear that up:** 그걸 깨끗하게 하다 / **in no time:** 바로

That's all? Why didn't you just say so! I know a dermatologist that can clear that up in no time.
그게 다야? 그럼 그렇다고 말을 하지! 그거 바로 치료해줄 수 있는 피부과 의사 아는데.

More to Talk!

 피부 관리에 관한 표현

My chin keeps breaking out! 내 턱에 계속 뭐가 나.

My mom keeps her skin healthy by getting an exfoliating massage at the bath house. 우리 엄마는 공중 목욕탕에서 때를 밀어 피부를 건강하게 유지한다.

There is a new cream on the market that is supposed to reduce age spots. 노인성 반점을 줄일 수 있는 새로운 크림이 출시되어 있다.

I'm thinking about getting a little work done on my face. 얼굴에 뭔가 하려고 생각 중이다.

Everyone likes a white complexion but I prefer darker skin. 다들 하얀 피부를 좋아하지만 난 구릿빛 피부를 선호해.

ChitChat 020

You've got to look the part.
거기에 어울리게 보여야지.

 King_Michael

Nice profile pic.
프로필 사진 멋진데.

겜폐남

Thanks. Do I look like a professional or what? Lol
고마워. 나 진짜 프로처럼 보이지 않냐? ㅋㅋ

 King_Michael

🎵 **n**: and의 약자

I'm shocked to see you out of a t-shirt n sneakers.
티셔츠와 운동화에서 벗어난 니 모습을 보고 쇼크 받았어.

🎵 **suit**: 아래위 한 벌의 양복 (정장)

겜폐남

Heh. But what do you think of the suit?
헤. 근데 그 양복 어때?

 King_Michael

🎵 **top notch**: 최고의, 일류의

Top notch.
최고!

🎵 **go well together**: 잘 어울리다

겜폐남

And the tie? Do they go well together?
글고 타이는? 잘 어울릴까?

King_Michael   🎵 since when?: 언제부터? / this stuff: 이런 거

The whole ensemble looks great. Since when did you care so much about this stuff?
전체 앙상블이 멋지다. 언제부터 이런 거에 신경 썼니?

🎵 get serious about: ~에 진지해지다   겜폐남

I decided it's time to get serious about getting a job. And if you want a good job you've got to look the part.
취업에 진지해질 때가 됐다고 결심했어. 좋은 직장을 원하면 거기에 어울리게 보여야지.

 King_Michael

Who are you?
누구냐 너?

🎵 raid: 급습, 기습   겜폐남

Huh?
엉?

 King_Michael   🎵 make the big money: 큰 돈 벌다

Nothing. So proud of you.
You'll be making the big money in no time.
암것도 아냐. 넘 자랑스럽다. 너 곧 떼돈 벌겠는데.

More to Talk!

 남성 패션에 관련된 표현

I got my dad a pair of cufflinks for his birthday. 아빠한테 생신선물로 커프스를 사드렸어.

They offer a shoe shining service as part of the hotel amenities. 그 호텔은 편의 시설의 일부로 구두 닦는 서비스를 제공해.

An expensive watch can be considered an investment. 비싼 시계는 투자로 생각하될 수 있어.

After you buy the suit you have to get it tailored. 양복을 구입한 다음에는 수선을 맡겨야 해.

He paired a corduroy blazer with jeans and it looked pretty good. 그는 골덴 자켓과 진을 매치시켰는데 썩 보기 좋더라.

ChitChat 021

I have NOTHING to wear. 입을 게 하.나.도. 없어.

 천사표

🎤 go to a wedding: 결혼식장에 가다

> ARGH. This is so frustrating! I'm going to a wedding this weekend and I have NOTHING to wear.
> 으아~~~, 미치겠다! 이번 주말에 결혼식에 가는데 입을 게 하나도 없어.

🎤 filled to capacity: 가득 차 있는

Kell2013

> What are you talking about? Your closet is filled to capacity.
> 무슨 말이야? 옷장에 잔뜩 있잖아.

 천사표

> It's all last season's stuff. I need something new.
> 몽땅 지난 시즌 거야. 새 옷 필요하다구.

🎤 first birthday party: 돌잔치

Kell2013

> What about that dress you wore to Haney's 1st birthday party?
> 하니의 돌잔치에 입었던 원피스는 어때?

 천사표

> I can't wear that again! Everyone has seen it!
> 그걸 또 입을 순 없지! 다들 이미 봤는데!

Kell2013

> That outfit you wore to brunch 2 weeks ago was also pretty cute.
> 2주 전에 브런치 먹을 때 입었던 옷도 꽤 예쁜던데.

 천사표

It's getting a little tight around the waist and the baby stained the blouse.
허리 부분이 좀 타이트해지고 아기 때문에 블라우스가 얼룩졌어.

🔖 stain: 얼룩지게 하다

Kell2013

You know what this means?
그렇다는 건 무슨 뜻인 줄 알지?

 천사표

Time to go shopping!!! :)
쇼핑 타임!!!

🔖 Are you in? (함께) 갈 거지?(할 거지?)

Kell2013

Everything is on sale right now, too! Hehe Are you in?
게다가 지금 몽땅 세일 중이야! 헤헤. 갈 거지?

 천사표

Yes, Ma'am!
네, 마님!

 쇼핑에 관한 표현

Everything in the store is on clearance. 상점에 있는 모든 상품은 땡처리 세일 중이야.

If you have a membership card you get a discount. 회원 카드를 소지하면 할인 받아.

They won't let you try on anything before you buy it. 거기서는 구매 전까지 아무것도 못 입어보게 해.

The offer is buy one get one free so I got one for my cousin too.
하나 사면 하나 더 준대서 사촌 것도 하나 생겼어.

Their return policy is very strict so be careful about what you buy.
거기 반품 규정이 엄격하니까 구매할 때 조심해.

You look fresh off the runway. 너 꼭 모델 같아.

 백조

Check me out!
나 좀 봐봐!

🎵 fresh off the runway: 런웨이에서 방금 나온   동분서주

Gorgeous! You look fresh off the runway!
예쁘다! 너 꼭 모델 같아!

빈

Oooh! Where'd you get that dress?
우~! 그 원피스는 어디서 샀니?

 백조

🎵 b/c: because / for a while: 잠시 동안

**Heh heh. It's cute right? It'd better be.
I'll be paying off my credit card for a while b/c of it.**
헤헤. 이쁘지, 그치? 예뻐야지. 이거 때문에 당분간 신용카드에서 돈 좀 빠져나갈 거야.

🎵 Oh, no: 안돼, 어떡해   동분서주

**Oh no. Did you really charge it?
You had finally paid down your old debt.**
어떡해. 정말 카드로 샀어? 예전에 빚진 거 이제야 다갚았잖아.

 백조

deserve: 마땅히 ~하다, ~할 자격이 있다

**Don't be a nag! lol I deserve nice things. :P
It's a present to myself for getting an internship.**
잔소리 좀 하지 마! ㅋㅋ. 난 좋은 것 좀 사도 돼. (메롱~) 인턴십 구했다고 나한테 주는 선물이야.

work hard to (get a position): (그 자리를 얻으려고) 애쓰다, 노력하다

동분서주

**Well then good for you.
You did work really hard to get that position.**
그렇담 잘했어. 거기 들어가려고 진짜 애썼잖아.

빈

And now she can start working harder to pay off that debt. :P
그리고 이제는 빚을 갚으려고 더 열심히 일할 수 있겠지 (메롱~)

동분서주

lollll
ㅋㅋㅋㅋ

 백조

Forget you guys!
얘들아, 됐거든!

스스로에게 한턱 내기

I worked hard and now I want to reward myself. 열심히 일했으니 이제 나한테 상을 줄 거야.

It's important to take care of the kids but don't forget to take care of yourself. 애들을 잘 돌보는 것은 중요하지만 자신을 돌보는 것도 잊어서는 안 된다.

I'm going to spoil myself with a spa package. 스파 패키지로 나 스스로를 대접할 거야.

Let's treat ourselves to a night on the town. 시내에 있는 나이트에 가서 실컷 놀아보자.

Devote a day to pampering yourself at least once a month. 적어도 한 달에 한번씩 하루를 스스로에게 한턱 내는 기분으로 써봐.

ChitChat 023

Isn't it too showy for the first date?
첫 데이트인데 너무 드러내는 거 아냐?

 동분서주
Help me out!
도와줘!

 천사표
?

 동분서주
Check this out.
이거 좀 봐.

동분서주

 천사표
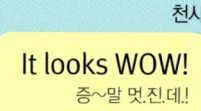
It looks WOW!
증~말 멋.진.데.!

동분서주
🎵 closet: 옷장
I searched through my closet all day to find it.
함 봐봐. 그거 찾느라 하루 종일 옷장을 뒤졌어.

 천사표
Haha. So, who's the lucky guy?
하하. 그 운 좋은 남자는 누규?

 동분서주 🎵 go out with ~: ~와 데이트 하러 나가다 / tonite: tonight의 약자
Hyun. I'm going out with him tonite.
현이야. 오늘 밤 그와 데이트가 있어.

 천사표
Hyun? Hyun, the hot lawyer????
현? 그 섹시한 변호사 현 말야?

동분서주
Correct.
정답

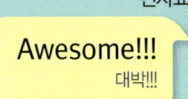 천사표
Awesome!!!
대박!!!

 동분서주
So, how do you like it?
그니까, 그 옷 어때?

 천사표
Nice.
멋져.

동분서주
🎵 showy: 드러내는, 노출이 심한
Uhmm... isn't it too showy for the 1st date?
첫 데이트인데 너무 드러내는 것 같진 않고?

 천사표
Personally I don't think it's too much.
갠적으론 과하다 생각 안 해.

 동분서주
🎵 get a 2nd opinion: 다른 사람의 의견을 구하다
Maybe I should get a 2nd opinion.
딴 사람 의견도 들어봐야겠다.

More to Talk!

 의복에 관한 표현

Guys like to show off their well-toned muscles by wearing tight clothes.
남자들은 꽉 끼는 옷을 입고 발달된 근육을 자랑하길 좋아해.

After the 3-day crash diet, she's ready to wear something skimpy.
3일간의 속성 다이어트 후, 그녀는 노출이 심한 옷을 입을 준비가 되었다.

Thick makeup doesn't go well with her clean-cut outfit. 진한 화장은 그녀의 단정한 의상과 어울리지 않는다.

Let me give you one important tip for appropriate business attire.
적절한 비즈니스 의상에 대해 중요한 팁 하나 줄게.

I felt like I was underdressed for the party. 그 파티에 옷을 너무 초라하게 입은 것 같은 기분이 들었다.

 ChitChat 024

I look like I just rolled out of bed.
나 완전 부스스해 보이네.

Kell2013

🎵 on one's way: 가고 있는, 곧 도착하는

Put your shoes on! I'm on my way over.
신발 신어! 금방 간다.

🎵 Wha: what과 같은 표현, 잉, 뭐   백조

Wha? Seriously?
잉? 정말?

Kell2013

Yeah. I'm almost there. About 5 minutes away.
응. 거의 왔어. 5분쯤 걸려.

백조

No! I have to take a shower! Come by later.
안돼! 샤워해야 해! 나중에 와.

Kell2013

🎵 throw on: 적당히 아무거나 입다, 대충 걸치다

No can do. I've got plans later. Just throw something on.
그럴 순 없어. 나중에 약속이 있거든. 걍 대충 입어.

64 SNS 잉글리시 톡

🎧 **not suitable for innocent eyes:** (모습이 끔찍해서) 다른 사람 보기에 민망한   백조

> It's just you that's coming, right? I'm not suitable for innocent eyes.
> 너만 오는 거지, 그치? 남한테 보여줄 몰골이 아니야.

 Kell2013

> 천사표 is with me!
> 천사표랑 같이 가는데!

🎧 **rolled out of bed:** 부스스한(침대에서 방금 일어난 듯한)   백조

> Are you kidding? I look like I just rolled out of bed. Gimme some time!
> 농담하냐? 나 완전 부스스해. 시간 좀 줘!

 Kell2013

> Alright then we'll stop by in 20.
> 알았어. 그럼 20분 정도 있다 들를게.

백조
> K. See u in 20.
> 오케이. 20분 있다가 보자.

 준비에 관련된 표현

More to Talk!

I need to get changed before we go. 출발하기 전에 옷 갈아입어야 해.

Do these shoes match my outfit? 이 신발이 내 옷과 어울려?

I have the perfect earrings to go with that necklace. 그 목걸이와 잘 어울리는 완벽한 귀걸이가 있어.

I pulled this outfit together in five minutes. 5분 만에 이 의상을 갖춰 입었다.

Can you help me pick something to wear? 입을 것 좀 같이 골라줄래?

 025

What's your point?
하고 싶은 말이 뭐야?

 천사표
> What's your ideal type of guy?
> 어떤 남자가 이상형이야?

 Kell2013
> Oh dear. Why are you asking again?
> 아이구. 왜 또 물어봐?

 천사표
> Tell me!
> 말해봐!

 Kell2013
> Beggars can't be choosers...
> 가릴 형편이 아니잖아…

천사표
> ROFL You're really not going to share?
> 빵터짐. 정말 말 안해줄 거야?

✏️ What's your point?: 요점이 뭐야? 하고 싶은 말이 뭐야?

 Kell2013
> Seriously, what's your point?
> 진짜로, 무슨 말을 하려고 그래?

 천사표
> I'm looking for someone to set you up with.
> 너랑 소개시켜 줄 사람 찾고 있거든.

Kell2013

Uhmmm... If you say so.
음…..정 그렇다면…

 천사표

So?
그렇다면?

 Kell2013

Tall, dark, well-built, nice butt...
큰 키, 구릿빛 피부, 단단한 체구, 섹시한 엉덩이에…

 천사표

Hehe. Would that be all? ;)
헤헤. 그게 다야?

 Kell2013

Of course not. The list goes on. Irresistibly handsome with a cute smile that kills me... filthy rich...
물론 아니지. 더 있지. 살인 미소에 무지무지 잘생긴데다, 돈은 더럽게 많고…

 천사표

Now I get why you're still single. :P
이제야 왜 아직 싱글인지 알겠다. (메롱)

 More to Talk!

 외모와 관련된 표현

You look much younger than your age. 넌 나이보다 훨씬 동안이야.
He's over 40, but looks half his age. 그는 40이 넘었지만 자기 나이의 절반으로 보인다.
You always look neat and well-groomed. 넌 늘 깔끔하고 단정해 보여.
He has very good taste in fashion. 그는 패션 감각이 정말 뛰어나.
He's going bald in his mid-twenties. 그는 20대 중반에 탈모가 진행되고 있어.

CHAT 02 **67**

Review — Words & Expressions — CHAT 02

ChitChat 015 p 46
You should call ahead for an appointment.

squeeze someone in ~를 끼워넣어 주다
at the last minute 막판에
flawless 완벽한
affordable 알맞은, 저렴한
while I'm at it 내친 김에
You should call ahead to make an appointment. 예약하려면 미리 전화해야 해.
get a pedi 페디큐어 (관리)받다
pedi(pedicure) 페디큐어
twice a month 한 달에 두 번
remove dead skin 각질제거 하다
dead skin 각질
pain 귀찮음, 고통
after a while 한동안
tag along 따라 가다
Make it for two. 두 명으로 해줘.
walk-in customers 예약 안하고 가는 손님
fully booked 예약이 꽉 찬

ChitChat 016 p 48
How about bangs?

hair salon 미용실
get a perm 파마하다
pick on ~ ~를 괴롭히다, 트집잡다
hairdo 헤어 스타일
do the magic 마법을 부리다, 마술처럼 작용하다
How about bangs? 앞머리를 자르는 게 어때?
bangs 앞머리를 가지런히 짧게 자름

It'll take 10 years off of you. (그렇게 하면) 10년은 더 어려 보일 거야.
get one's hair straightened 스트레이트 파마하다
trim one's hair 머리 길이를 다듬다
itchy 가려운
scalp 두피

ChitChat 017 p 50
I went a little too far…

grab a bite 간단히 먹다
blond 금발의
dye 염색하다
main character 주인공
copy one's style ~의 스타일을 따라하다
I went a little too far. 좀 오버했어.
There's not a thing you could do. 네가 할 수 있는 일은 하나도 없다, 네가 ~할 리가 없다.
throw on 대충 걸치다
shoulder length 어깨 길이
massage one's scalp 두피 마사지하다
for years 수 년 동안, 몇 년간
color one's hair 염색하다

ChitChat 018 p 52
I couldn't even recognize her!

recognize 알아보다
I couldn't even recognize her. 그녀를 알아보지도 못하겠더라.
lose weight 살 빠지다
on top of that 게다가
multiple 다수의, 수없이 많은

CHAT 02

plastic surgery 성형 수술
undergo a plastic surgery 성형 수술을 하다
I'm speechless. 할 말을 잃었어.
thing is… 문제는…, 실은….
full of oneself 거만한
have a work done 성형 수술하다
get a massage 마사지 받다
get a nose job 코 수술하다
get facial Botox injections 얼굴에 보톡스 주사 맞다
eyeliner 아이라이너

ChitChat 019 p 54
I can't get rid of this backne.

Spill. 털어놔, 얘기 해.
bathing suit 수영복
self-conscious 자의식이 강한, 남의 눈을 의식하는
skinny 마른, 날씬한
immaculate 무결한
get rid of 없애다
backne 등에 난 여드름, 등드름
I can't get rid of this backne. 이 등드름을 없앨 수가 없어.
dermatologist 피부과 의사
clear something up 깨끗하게 하다
in no time 바로, 금방
get an exfoliating massage 때밀다
bath house 공중 목욕탕
on the market 시장에 나와 있는, 출시된
age spots 노인성 반점
complexion 안색, 피부색

ChitChat 020 p 56
You've got to look the part.

top notch 최고의, 일류의
go well 잘 어울리다
get serious about ~ ~에 대해 진지해지다
look the part 그 역할에 어울리다. 그 위치에 어울리다
proud 자랑스러운
make the big money 큰 돈 벌다
shoe shining service 구두닦이 서비스

ChitChat 021 p 58
I have NOTHING to wear.

go to a wedding 결혼식에 가다
I have nothing to wear. 난 아무것도 입을 게 없다.
filled to capacity 가득 차 있는
first birthday party 돌잔치
outfit 의상
stain 얼룩지다
Are you in? 함께 할 거지?, 낄 거지?
clearance 땡 처리 세일
get a discount 할인 받다
return policy 반품 규정

ChitChat 022 p 60
You look fresh off the runway.

fresh off the runway 런웨이에서 방금 나온
It'd better be. 그래야 할 거야.
pay off 상환하다, 갚다
for a while 잠시 동안

debt 빚
nag 잔소리
Don't be a nag. 잔소리 좀 하지 마.
deserve 마땅히 ~하다, ~할 자격이 있다
treat oneself 스스로에게 잘해주다

ChitChat 023   p 62
Isn't it too showy for the first date?

search through 샅샅이 뒤지다
Who's the lucky guy? 그 운 좋은 남자는 누구야?
showy 드러낸, 노출이 있는
It's too much 그거 과하다, 심하다
get a second opinion 딴 사람의 의견을 들어보다
show off 자랑하다
well-toned 잘 발달된
crash diet 속성 다이어트
skimpy 노출이 심한
clean-cut 단정한
attire 복장, 의상
underdressed 초라한, 신경 쓰지 않은 듯한 복장의

ChitChat 024   p 64
I look like I just rolled out of bed.

on my way 가고 있는 중인
come by later 나중에 들르다
No can do. 안돼. 그럴 순 없어.
throw on 대충 걸치다
suitable 적절한
innocent 순진한
not suitable for innocent eyes (모습이) 너무 끔찍해서 다른 사람 보기에 민망한
I look like I just rolled out of bed. 나 완전 부스스해 보여.
get changed 옷 갈아입다

ChitChat 025   p 66
What's your point?

Beggars can't be choosers. 이것저것 가릴 형편이 아니다.
What's your point? 하고 싶은 말이 뭐야?
If you say so. 정 그렇다면.
well-built 체격이 좋은
butt 엉덩이
The list goes on. 리스트는 계속된다.
irresistibly 참을 수 없을 정도로
look half one's age 나이의 절반으로 보인다, 너무 젊어 보인다
well-groomed 단정한
have a good taste 감각이 뛰어나다
go bald 탈모가 진행되다
in one's mid-twenties 20대 중반에

CHAT 03

Love
사랑

- 026 Love is one thing and marriage is another.
- 027 It's not like I have a ring on my finger.
- 028 She won't give me the time of day.
- 029 What's with you lately?
- 030 Pull yourself together.
- 031 It was a total disaster!
- 032 Epic fail
- 033 It's just not working.
- 034 Friendship between men and women is impossible. Period.
- 035 Two-timing is not my thing.
- 036 I made a faux pas.
- 037 He's still hung up on his ex.

ChitChat 026

Love is one thing and marriage is another.
사랑과 결혼은 별개지.

Jas

🔖 sign up with ~: ~에 가입하다

I signed up with a professional matchmaking agency.
결혼 전문 업체에 가입했어.

Kell2013

You did WHAT???
"뭘" 했다고???

Jas

🔖 decent: 괜찮은, (인간성) 좋은

I decided to get some professional help finding a decent girl.
괜찮은 여자 찾는 데 전문가의 도움을 받기로 했다고.

🔖 go for: 좋아하다, 선호하다   Kell2013

I thought that's the last thing you'd go for?
그런 건 절대 취향 아닌 줄 알았는데?

Jas

I think it'll be more practical.
그게 더 실용적일 거 같아.

🔖 go out with ~: ~와 데이트하다   Kell2013

What about all the girls you went out with?
데이트하던 여자들은 모두 어쩌고?

Jas

🎵 **A is one thing and B is another:** A와 B는 별개이다

Love is one thing and marriage is another.
사랑과 결혼은 별개지.

 🎵 **calculating:** 계산적인 Kell2013

Sounds TOO calculating.
너~무 계산적인데.

 Jas

I'm super busy with work and...
내 일이 워낙 정신없이 바쁘니까...

🎵 **arrange:** 주선하다 Kell2013

... and they keep arranging dates for you?
그래서 업체에서 계속 알아서 상대를 소개시켜주고?

 Jas

That's it. This way I can focus on my work.
그거지. 이렇게 하면 난 일에만 열중할 수 있고.

🎵 **win-win situation:** 윈윈 상황, 꿩도 먹고 알도 먹고 Kell2013

So it's a win-win situation for you.
그니까 너한텐 윈윈이네.

More to Talk!

 이성 간의 만남 관련 표현 1

I was on a blind date. 나 소개팅 했어.

I'll ask him out tomorrow. 내일 그에게 데이트 신청할 거야.

Would you prefer love marriage or arranged marriage? 연애결혼과 중매결혼 중 어느 편이 더 좋아?

She'll break up with him. 그녀는 그 남자와 헤어질 거야.

She got back together with him after all. 그녀는 결국 그 남자와 재결합했다.

It's not like I have a ring on my finger.

내 손가락에 반지라도 끼고 있는 것도 아니잖아.

빈

Who was that guy I just saw you with? :O
너랑 같이 있던 사람 누규?

백조
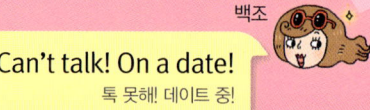

Can't talk! On a date!
톡 못해! 데이트 중!

빈

Whaaaaaaaaaaaat?! What happened to King_Michael? Isn't he your boyfriend anymore?
뭐어어어어엇?! King_Michal은 어쩌고? 이젠 남친 아냐?

백조

:P
메롱~

빈

I thought you two had something going on. Am I wrong?
너네 둘 사이에 뭔가 있는 거 같았는데. 아니니?

백조
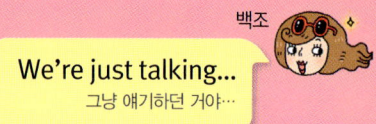

We're just talking...
그냥 얘기하던 거야…

빈

More than talking!
얘기하는 거 이상이던데!

백조

Yeah but it's not like I have a ring on my finger.
마쟈. 하지만 내 손가락에 반지라도 끼고 있는 것도 아니잖아.

빈

I am so out of the loop!
We need to grab a coffee and have some serious girl talk.
너무 소외감 느끼네! 커피 한잔 하면서 여자들끼리 제대로 수다 좀 떨어보자.

백조

Haha True. Gotta go! Call u later. ;)
하하. 맞아. 가야 해! 나중에 전화할게. ;)

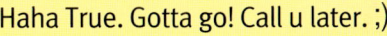

More to Talk!

 이성 간의 만남 관련 표현2

You two seem pretty serious these days. 너네 둘 요즘 꽤 진지해 보이던데.

We are not exclusive; I'm seeing other guys. 우리 사귀는 거 아냐. 난 다른 사람들도 만나보고 있어.

I'm not ready to settle down with one girl. 난 한 여자에게 정착할 준비가 안 되어 있어.

I'm a "one-woman" kind of guy. 난 "한 여자"만 사귀는 그런 남자야.

I'm looking for a serious, committed relationship. 난 진지하게, 올인하는 관계를 찾고 있어.

She won't give me the time of day.
그녀는 날 거들떠보지도 않을 거야.

겜폐남

Can I ask you something? I need your advice.
뭐 물어봐도 돼? 조언이 필요해.

Tae
Shoot.
해.

겜폐남

It's 빈.
빈 얘기야.

Tae
What about her?
걔 뭐?

겜폐남

She won't give me the time of day.
걘 날 거들떠보지도 않을 거야.

Tae
Wait a minute...
잠깐...

겜폐남

I've tried everything.
별 거 다 해봤어.

✎ have a crush on ~ : ~에 반해 있다, ~한테 푹 빠지다

Tae
Are you telling me that you have a crush on 빈?!??!
니가 빈한테 홀딱 빠졌단 얘기야?

겜폐남

I thought you knew. I thought everyone knew.
아는 줄 알았는데. 딴 사람들도 다.

♪little brother: 남동생 Tae

 **I guess it's about time I started teaching my little brother about the ladies.**
이제야 우리 남동생한테 여자에 대해 한 수 가르쳐 줄 때가 된 거 같군.

 겜폐남 ♪Don't patronize.: 가르치려 들지 마, 생색 좀 내지 마, 잘난 척은.

Don't patronize. Just help.
잘난 척은. 좀 도와줘.

♪Gimme a call tonite.: Give me a call tonight.의 구어 표현, 오늘 밤에 나한테 전화해. Tae

Alright, alright. Gimmie a call tonite and we'll talk.
알아, 알았쓰. 오늘 밤에 전화해서 얘기하자.

 겜폐남 ♪Thanx: Thanks의 인터넷 표현

Thanx!
고마워!

 More to Talk!

 이성 간의 만남 관련 표현 3

I didn't know you had feelings for her! 그 여자한테 맘이 있는지 몰랐어!
He is always going on about her, I think it's a crush. 그 남자는 늘 그 여자 얘기만 한다. 반한 거 같아.
My little sister has a thing for her tutor. 내 막내 여동생은 과외 선생님을 좋아한다..
I think they are more than just friends. 난 걔들이 그저 친구 이상이라고 생각해.
The two of them seem awfully close for just "friends". 걔네 둘 그냥 "친구"라고 하기엔 심하게 가까운 거 같아.

CHAT 03 **77**

What's with you lately?
요즘 왜 그래?

겜폐남
Where you been, bro?
어딨었어, 친구?

King_Michael
Around...
근처에...

 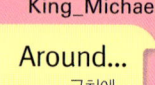

겜폐남
You never come out anymore.
Haven't seen much of you online either.
너 절대 안 나오더라. 온라인에서도 잘 안 보이고.

King_Michael
Just busy.
그냥 바빠서.

겜폐남
You've never been too busy for just a drink.
What's with you lately?
술 한 잔도 못할 만큼 바쁜 적 없었잖아. 요즘 왜 그래?

🎵 return one's calls: ~에게 회신하다

King_Michael
I think 백조 has moved on. She stopped returning my calls.
백조랑 완전히 끝난 거 같아. 내 전화에 회신을 안 하네.

겜폐남
Maybe she's busy too?
걔도 바쁠 수도?

✏ answer one's texts: 문자에 답하다   King_Michael
She won't answer my texts either. She doesn't even check them.
문자도 씹고 있어. 확인조차 안 하는 거 같아.

 겜폐남
Ah...
아…

King_Michael
What do you think I should do?
어떻게 할까?

 겜폐남
I guess you'd better forget her. Join me at the PC room?
잊는 게 나을 듯. PC 방에서 만날까?

King_Michael
...

More to Talk!

 이별 조짐에 관한 표현

You never respond to my messages! 너 내 메시지에 절대 답장 안하더라!
Are you ignoring me? 나 무시하는 거야?
She hung up on me and turned off her phone. 그녀는 내 전화를 (도중에) 끊고 전원을 꺼버렸어.
He barely even calls me anymore. 그는 이젠 더 이상 전화조차 잘 안해.
I don't think he is interested in me. 그 남자 나한테 관심 없나 봐.

CHAT 03 **79**

ChitChat 030

Pull yourself together.
좀 추슬러봐

동분서주
OMG! OMG! OMG!
세상에나! 세상에나! 세상에나!

Kell2013
What happened?
왜 그래?

동분서주 — make a mistake: 실수하다
I made a terrible mistake.
나 완전 실수했어.

Kell2013
What?
무슨?

동분서주 — be exclusive: 사귀다, 둘이 만나다
I asked Hyun to be exclusive.
현한테 사귀자고 말했어.

make the first move: 먼저 시작하다, 먼저 행동을 취하다

Kell2013
Wow! YOU made the first move!
와우, 니가 먼저 행동 개시했네!

동분서주 — go out of one's mind: 제정신이 아니다
I must have gone out of my mind!!!
정신 나갔나 봐!!!

Kell2013
It doesn't always have to be the guy.
꼭 남자들만 그러란 법 없잖아.

동분서주
Oh, I can't even breathe!!!
오, 나 숨도 못 쉬겠어!!!

Kell2013
🔖 **pull oneself together:** 정신 차리다, 추스르다
Relax. Pull yourself together.
진정해. 좀 추슬러봐.

 동분서주
🔖 **regret -ing:** ~한 것을 후회하다
I'm already regretting asking him like that.
괜히 말한 거 벌써 후회가 돼.

Kell2013
Don't.
그러지 마.

 동분서주
Yeah. I just did what I had to do.
그래. 난 그저 해야 할 일을 한 것뿐야.

동분서주
🔖 **go on:** 전진하다, 지속하다
I couldn't go on not telling him.
말 안하곤 못 살았을 거야.

Kell2013
 **Good. Good.**
잘했어. 잘했어.

More to Talk!

 후회에 관련된 표현

I shouldn't have said that. 그 말을 하지 말았어야 했는데.
Stop regretting your decision. 이미 내린 결정에 대해 후회하지 마.
I feel really sorry for not seeing you one last time. 마지막으로 널 못 봐서 정말 유감이야.
I'm terribly sorry for being careless. 경솔하게 굴어서 정말 미안해.
Regret over wasted time is more wasted time. 시간 낭비했다고 후회하는 게 더욱 시간 낭비야.

It was a total disaster!
완전 끔찍했어!

Kell2013 set A up with B A와 B가 만나도록 자리를 마련하다, 소개팅을 주선하다

I heard 천사표 set you up with a girl.
천사표가 소개팅시켜줬다며?

Yup: Yes의 구어체   Jas

Yup.
응.

Kell2013

How'd it go?
어떻게 됐어?

disaster: 재난, 재앙   Jas

It was a total disaster.
완전 끔찍했어.

Kell2013

Too bad.
안됐다.

talk my ear off that ~: 내 귀가 아프게 ~라고 말하다 / hot: 예쁜, 섹시한   Jas

천사표 talked my ear off saying that she was hot.
귀가 닳도록 그 여자가 예쁘다고 하더니.

Kell2013 ur: your의 인터넷 약자 / r: are의 인터넷 약자

Maybe ur standards r way too high.
니 기대치가 너무 높은 거겠지.

🎵 have a conversation with ~: ~와 대화를 나누다   Jas

I just want someone that I can have a nice conversation with.
그냥 말이 잘 통하는 사람이면 되는데.

 Kell2013

Ha!
흥!

🎵 reject: 거부하다, 거절하다 / hottie: 예쁜 여자   Jas

But who would reject a hottie?
그래도 예쁜 여자를 누가 거절하겠니?

 Kell2013   🎵 shallow: 속물의, 속이 빤히 보이는

Ugh. How shallow!
웩, 속물!

**More to Talk!**

 일의 진척 상황을 나타내는 표현

How's it going? 어떻게 되어 가니?
It was easier than I thought. 생각보다 쉬웠어.
We feel stuck with no way out. 우린 오도가도 못하고 막힌 거 같아.
Well, the worst part is over. 글쎄, 최악의 고비는 넘겼어.
I'm sure we can make it one way or another. 우린 그럭저럭 해낼 수 있을 거라 믿어.

ChitChat 032

Epic fail 대박 사고

겜폐남
I give up on women.
여자들 포기했어.

Tae
lol Why's that?
ㅋㅋ 그건 왜?

겜폐남
I just have no idea how to impress them.
호감을 주는 법을 도무지 모르겠어.

Tae
Things didn't go well with 빈? Didn't you follow my advice?
빈하고 잘 안됐어? 내 충고대로 안했어?

겜폐남
I made a fool of myself. I did like you said. I told her I was interested in what she's interested in.
바보인증했어. 니 말대로 했는데. 걔가 좋아하는 거 나도 좋아한다고 했거든.

Tae
Which is?
그게 뭔데?

겜폐남
🔖 fancy-schmancy: fancy와 schmancy가 운율이 같아 붙여 씀. 엄청나게 화려한
Coffee. So I went to her café and ordered some fancy-schmancy drink. But the thing was so bitter I could barely drink it.
커피. 걔가 일하는 카페에 가서 휘황찬란한 음료수를 시켰어. 근데 그게 넘 써서 못 마시겠는 거야.

♪SMH: shaking my head의 약어, 고개를 절레절레 흔드는 동작   Tae

And she saw this? SMH...
그래서 걔가 봤어? 절레절레..

 겜폐남

Yeah I caught her looking at me. So I got really nervous and knocked the glass over. It shattered everywhere.
어. 날 쳐다보더라. 그래서 넘 긴장해서 그만 잔을 넘어뜨렸어. 그게 온 사방으로 깨어버렸어.

Tae

Fail.
사고쳤군.

 겜폐남

Then her boss came out screaming at her for having her friends wreck the place.
그랬더니 걔 보스가 나와서 걔 친구들이 카페를 엉망으로 만든다고 고함을 쳤어.

Tae

Whoa... Epic fail. You're right to give up.lol
후아…. 대박 사고네. 포기 잘 했어 ㅋㅋㅋ

More to Talk!

 굴욕과 관계되는 표현

She probably thinks I'm a complete idiot. 그 여잔 아마 내가 완전히 멍청이라고 생각할 거야.
I'm not just embarrassed, I'm mortified! 그저 당황한 정도가 아니라 완전 굴욕이었어!
I can never show my face there again. 다시는 거기에 얼굴 비치지 않을 거야.
Can you believe he did that? What a clown! 그가 그랬다는 게 믿어져? 바보 같이!
It was so humiliating. I never want to do it again! 굴욕이었어. 다신 안할 거야!

ChitChat 033

It's just not working.
안 되겠어.

King_Michael 🔖 answer one's messages: ~의 메시지에 회답하다

Why aren't you answering my messages?
내 메시지 왜 씹냐?

Things are really crazy lately. Sorry.
요즘 완전 미친 듯 바빴어. 미안

King_Michael

It seems like you're not interested in me anymore.
나한테 더 이상 관심 없나 봐.

...

King_Michael

You don't have anything to say?
할 말 없어?

We need to talk. Want to meet next weekend?
얘기 좀 하자. 담 주말에 만날까?

King_Michael

Seriously? Next weekend? Don't you think that's a little late?
정말? 담 주말? 좀 늦는 것 같지 않아?

백조

Listen, Michael. It's just not working.
잘 들어. 마이클. 우린 안 되겠어.

King_Michael

You're breaking up with me by text message?
너 나랑 문자로 헤어지잔 거야?

백조

Sorry.
미안.

King_Michael whatever: 그러시든지, 그러거나 말거나, 알 게 뭐야

Whatever.
그러시든지.

 이별에 관련된 표현

Can't we just start over? 다시 시작할 수 없을까?
Just give me another chance. 한 번만 더 기회를 줘.
I'm still really into you. 아직도 나 너 정말 좋아해.
We can't work it out. 우린 안돼.
I'm not going to give you up without a fight. 싸우지도 않고 널 포기하진 않을 거야.

ChitChat 034

Friendship between men and women is impossible. Period.

남녀 간의 우정은 불가능해. 끝.

동분서주
I need a guy's point of view.
남자 입장에서 얘기해줘.

Jas
Ok.
그래.

동분서주
Sue's boss wants her to join him on his biz trip.
수의 사장이 같이 출장을 가자고 한대.

Jas
Where is he going?
어디로 가는데?

동분서주
*be into ~: ~을 좋아하다, ~에 관심이 많다
Canada. I think he's pretty into her.
캐나다. 그 사장이 걔를 꽤 좋아하는 거 같아.

Jas
Maybe he just considers her a coworker or friend?
그냥 동료나 친구로 생각하는 거 아냐?

동분서주
Friendship between men and women is impossible. Period.
남녀 간엔 우정은 없어. 끝.

Jas
Why not?
왜 없어?

동분서주
It's like cats and dogs. They can't be friends!
개와 고양이와 같은 이치지. 친구가 될 수 없다니깐!

Jas
But they can be lovers?
근데 애인은 되고?

동분서주
You know what I mean!!
내 말 알면서!

Jas

 whatever: 그렇담 뭐. 그러거나 말거나

**Well, whatever.
Just don't forget to fill me in on the details!**
그럼 뭐. 글고 자세한 뒷얘기 꼭 해줘.

동분서주
Sure ;)
고럼(찡긋)

More to Talk!

정보 공유에 관련된 표현

That's what I'm curious about. 그게 바로 내가 궁금한 점이야.

Be cautious when posting personal information online. 온라인에 개인정보를 게시할 때는 조심해.

Tell me how it happened in the first place. 애초에 그 일이 어떻게 일어났는지 얘기해줘.

I really wanna remove my personal info from the website. 그 웹사이트에 있는 내 개인 정보를 꼭 식제하고 싶어.

Teenagers tend to share too much info on FB. 10대들은 페이스북에 지나치게 많은 정보를 공유하는 경향이 있어.

 **ChitChat** 035

Two-timing is not my thing. 난 바람 피울 사람이 못돼.

동분서주
Let's break up.
헤어지자.

천사표
What????
뭐????

동분서주
♪ compatible: 서로 어울리는
We're not compatible.
우린 안 맞아.

♪ Knock it off: 집어치워, 그만 둬
천사표
Knock it off!
집어치워!

동분서주
♪ mess up: 헤매다, 망치다
I'm rehearsing these things so I don't mess up.
헤매지 않으려고 리허설 하는 중야.

천사표
What's with you?
왜 이래?

동분서주
You know I've been dating Hyun right?
내가 요즘 현이랑 만나는 거 알지?

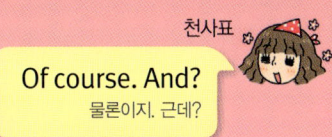
천사표

Of course. And?
물론이지. 근데?

동분서주

🎵 **on a date:** 데이트 중인

I saw him on a date with some other girl.
딴 여자랑 데이트하는 거 봤어.

🎵 **no way:** 말도 안돼, 절대 안돼

천사표
No way!!! Such a player!
말도 안돼!!! 선수구나!

동분서주

Maybe I should cheat to get back at him.
맞바람이라도 피울까 봐.

🎵 **Go for it:** 덤벼봐, 질러

천사표
Go for it!!!
질러버려!!!

동분서주

🎵 **~is not my thing:** 난 ~할 타입이 아냐, 난 ~할 사람이 아냐

No, two-timing is not my thing.
아냐. 난 바람 피울 사람이 아냐.

More to Talk!

제재와 관련된 표현

Cut it out. 그만 좀 해.
Stop it. 관둬.
Cut the crap. 헛소리하지 마.
Stay away. 떨어져.
Move. 비켜
Get off of me. 저리 비켜

ChitChat 036

I made a faux pas.
나 실수했어.

빈
You're not going to stop laughing when I tell you this.
내가 이 얘기 하면 넌 웃음을 멈출 수가 없을 거야.

백조
Tell me what?
뭔데 그래?

faux pas: (사회적) 실수 (프랑스어에서 나온 말)

빈
Let's just say I made a faux pas.
실수했다고나 할까.

백조
Spill.
말해.

chat up: (흑심을 갖고) 말 걸다, (이성에게) 수작을 부리다

빈
So, my nightmare boss...
I wanted to see if I could chat him up a little.
그니까, 악몽 같은 내 상사 말이야. 그 사람하고 좀 말이나 나눠보려 했거든.

jerk: 재수없는 사람(가벼운 욕)

백조
WHAT?! WHY?! He's such a jerk!
뭐?! 왜?! 완전 재수라며?

figure: 생각하다, 계산하다

빈
Yeah but he's a hot jerk. And I figured maybe he would start being nicer.
그래, 하지만 섹시한 재수거든. 글고 그가 좀 나이스해지지 않을까 생각했지.

 백조

I knew you had a crush on him. Well???
니가 그 사람한테 홀딱 반한 줄은 알고 있었지. 근데???

 빈

🔍 flirt with ~: ~와 시시덕거리다, ~에게 추파를 던지다

I was flirting with him when we were closing up the café. I must have been out of my mind. And then he had a piece of fuzz on his shirt.
카페 닫을 때 내가 시시덕거렸어. 내가 미쳤었나 봐. 근데 그 남자 셔츠에 보풀이 묻어 있는 거야.

 백조

🔍 pick something off: ~를 떼주다

So... you picked it off? lol
그래서… 그걸 떼 줬어? 빵터짐

 빈

And I heard a noise. When I turned around there was a woman at the door. His WIFE!
근데 소리가 들렸어. 뒤돌아보니까 문간에 여자가 있더라. 부인이었어!

 백조

🔍 You can't make things like this up!: 이런 건 지어낼 수 없는 거야, 설마 뻥이겠지!

lolllllllllllllll You can't make things like this up!
ㅋㅋㅋㅋㅋㅋㅋ 설마 뻥이겠지!

More to Talk!

 사회 생활 & 에티켓에 관한 표현

Smoking in front of your boss is bad manners. 상사 앞에서 담배 피우는 것은 예의에 어긋난다.

It's inappropriate to wear miniskirts to work. 회사에서 미니스커트를 입는 것은 부적절하다.

Being late is rude but being too early is also a bad idea. 지각은 무례하지만 너무 일찍 가는 것도 좋은 생각이 아니다.

Bringing a gift for the host or hostess is proper etiquette. 초대받은 집에는 선물을 가져가는 것이 에티켓이다.

If you can't make it then you should at least call. 못 간다면 적어도 전화는 해야 한다.

ChitChat 037

He's still hung up on his ex.
그는 아직도 구여친에 연연해하고 있어.

Tae

What's with King_Michael? He seems really bummed lately.
King_Michael 왜 저래? 요즘 완전 저기압인데.

♪ hung up on ~ : ~에 연연해하는

He's still hung up on his ex. They broke up a few weeks ago and he can't seem to move on.
아직도 구여친에 연연해하고 있어. 몇 주 전에 헤어졌는데 잊혀지지 않나 봐.

Tae

♪ dang : damn의 완곡한 표현, 망할, 젠장

Dang. What happened?
망할. 무슨 일이야?

♪ dump : 차다, 버리다 / take it : 감수하다, 받아들이다

She dumped him by text. He didn't take it very well.
문자로 차버렸대. 받아들이기 힘든가 봐.

Tae

♪ sux : sucks의 줄임말

That sux. There's plenty of fish in the sea though.
완전 짜증나네. 뭐 여자가 개 하나뿐이냐.

I tried telling him that. He didn't appreciate it.
그렇게 말해주려고 했지. 고마워하지 않더라.

Tae

combo: combination의 약어

Hmm. Perhaps we should take him out this Sat. We can do the 4 spot combo.
흠. 이번 주 토요일에 걔 좀 데리고 나가자. 4차까지 콤보로 가는 거야.

겜폐남

4 spot combo?
4차까지 콤보라니?

 Tae

Samgyupsal, bar, club, singing room.
삼겹살, 술집, 클럽, 노래방

겜폐남

Hahaha. I'm down.
하하하. 내가 졌다.

 Tae

Alright I'll send him a text n see what he thinks.
좋아. 문자 쳐서 물어볼게.

겜폐남

Cool.
쪼아.

 유흥에 관한 표현

I'm sick of Hongdae. Let's go clubbing in Gangnam. 홍대 앞 지겨워. 강남에 클럽 가서 놀자.

That ritzy place in Apgujeong wasn't really my scene. 압구정에 있는 그 호화로운 곳은 별로 내 스탈 아니었어.

I'll get the next round if you go talk to that girl. 그 여자한테 가서 말 걸면 다음 차례는 내가 쏠게.

I'm tired of this place. Let's move to another spot. 여기 싫증나. 딴 데로 가자.

That place is full of hotties. 거기 물 너무 좋아.

Review   Words & Expressions   CHAT 03

ChitChat  026 p 72
Love is one thing and marriage is another.

sign up with ~ ~에 가입하다
matchmaking agency 결혼 정보 업체
decent 괜찮은, 좋은
go for ~을 좋아하다, 선호하다
practical 실용적인
go out with ~ ~와 데이트하다
Love is one thing and marriage is another. 사랑과 결혼은 별개지.
calculating 계산적인
super busy with ~ ~하느라 너무 바쁜
arrange 주선하다
focus on ~ ~에 집중하다
win-win situation 윈윈 상황
blind date 소개팅
ask someone out ~에게 데이트 신청하다
love marriage 연애결혼
arranged marriage 중매결혼
get back together 재결합하다

ChitChat  027 p 74
It's not like I have a ring on my finger.

on a date 데이트 중
It's not like I have a ring on my finger. 내 손가락에 반지라도 끼고 있는 건 아니잖아.
out of the loop 소외감 느끼는
grab a coffee 커피 한잔 하다

ChitChat  028 p 76

girl talk 여자끼리 나누는 수다
Gotta go! 가야해!
exclusive (이성 간에) 둘이만 사귀는
settle down 정착하다
committed relationship 올인하는 관계

She won't give me the time of day.

She won't give me the time of day.
그녀는 날 거들떠보지도 않을 거야.
have a crush 홀딱 반하다
crush 홀딱 반함
little brother 남동생
Don't patronize. 가르치려 들지 마, 생색 내지 마.
have feelings for~ ~에게 마음을 두고 있다
have a thing for~ ~에게 좋은 감정이 있다
more than just friends 친구 이상의 관계

ChitChat  029 p 78
What's with you lately?

bro brother, 친구
What's with you lately? 요즘 왜 그래?
return one's calls ~에게 회신하다
answer one's texts 문자에 답하다
respond to one's messages 문자에 답신하다
Are you ignoring me? 나 무시하는 거야?
hang up 전화를 끊다
turn off one's phone 전화기를 끄다

CHAT 03

ChitChat 030 — p 80
Pull yourself together.

make a mistake 실수하다
make the first move 먼저 행동 개시하다
out of one's mind 정신이 나간
breathe 숨쉬다
Pull yourself together. 좀 추슬러봐.
regret 후회하다
Stop regretting your decision. 이미 내린 결정에 대해 후회하지 마.
feel sorry for ~에 대해 유감으로 생각하다
one last time 마지막으로 한번
careless 경솔한
wasted time 시간 낭비

ChitChat 031 — p 82
It was a total disaster!

set someone up 소개팅 시켜주다
How'd it go? 어떻게 됐어?
It was a total disaster. 완전 끔찍했어.
talk one's ear off saying that ~ …의 귀가 닳도록 ~라고 말하다
way too high 지나치게 높은
have a conversation with ~와 이야기를 나누다
reject 거절하다
hottie 예쁜 여자
shallow 속물의
stuck 막힌, 오도가도 못하는
The worst part is over. 최악의 상황은 넘겼어.
one way or another 어떻게 해서든, 그럭저럭

ChitChat 032 — p 84
Epic fail

give up 포기하다
impress 감동 주다
follow one's advice 충고를 따르다
make a fool of oneself 바보짓 하다
fancy-schmancy 엄청 화려한
bitter 쓴
barely 겨우 ~한
knock 넘어뜨리다
shatter 산산조각나다
scream 소리지르다
wreck 망치다
epic fail 대박 사고
idiot 바보, 멍청이
mortified 굴욕적인
show one's face ~의 얼굴을 비치다 (나타나다)
What a clown! 어리석은 것!
humiliating 굴욕적인

ChitChat 033 — p 86
It's just not working.

lately 요즘, 최근에
It's just not working. 안되겠어.
break up with someone by text message 문자 메시지로 ~와 헤어지다
Whatever. 그러든지.
Can we start over? 우리 다시 시작할 수 있을까?
give someone another chance 다시 기회를 주다

without a fight 싸우지도 않고

ChitChat 034   p 88
Friendship between men and women is impossible. Period.

point of view 관점, 입장
biz trip 출장
be into ~ ~에 관심이 있다, 좋아하다
Friendship between men and women is impossible. Period. 남녀 사이에 우정은 불가능해. 이상.
It's like cats and dogs. 개와 고양이와 같은 이치야. 만나면 티격태격하는 사이야.
fill someone in on~ ~에 대해 …에게 설명하다, 말해주다
curious 궁금한
in the first place 애초에

ChitChat 035   p 90
Two-timing is not my thing.

compatible 잘 맞는, 서로 어울리는
knock it off 집어치워.
Such a player! 완전 선수구나!
cheat 바람 피우다, 속이다
get back at ~ ~에게 복수하다
Go for it! 질러!, 덤벼봐!
two-timing 양다리 걸치기
Two-timing is not my thing. 난 바람 피울 사람이 못돼.

ChitChat 036   p 92
I made a faux pas.

I made a faux pas. 나 (사회적으로) 실수했어.
nightmare 악몽
chat up 흑심을 갖고 말 걸다
jerk 재수없는 사람
flirt 시시덕거리다, 추파를 던지다
fuzz 보풀, 솜털
make up 만들어내다
inappropriate 부적절한

ChitChat 037   p 94
He's still hung up on his ex.

bummed 기운이 없는, 저기압의
ex 구여친, 구남친
He's still hung up on his ex. 그는 아직도 구여친에 연연해해.
move on 잊다(잊고 제 갈 길 가다)
dump 차다, 버리다
dump by text 문자로 차다
There's plenty of fish in the sea. 세상에 여자는 쌔고 쌨다.
take someone out ~를 데리고 나가다
spot 장소
combo combination의 줄인 표현
go clubbing 클럽가다
ritzy 호화로운
get the next round 다음 차례를 내다
I'll get the next round. 다음 차례는 내가 낸다.

CHAT 04
Health & Food
건강과 음식

- 038 Speak for yourself.
- 039 He lives off ramen and soda.
- 040 What exactly is that?
- 041 I'm not sure what she's into.
- 042 What should I eat to up my stamina?
- 043 I occasionally splurge on weekends.
- 044 The meat was dry and the veggies were all mushy.
- 045 Do they have any lo-cal options?
- 046 My stomach is growling.
- 047 What are you in the mood for?
- 048 You're hitting the gym pretty hard.
- 049 My head is killing me.
- 050 I'm quitting alcohol cold turkey!
- 051 I tripped while texting and walking.
- 052 My head feels foggy.
- 053 Worry can make you sick.
- 054 I'll keep my fingers crossed.
- 055 You'll be back to normal in no time.

 038

Speak for yourself.
사돈 남 말 하시네.

 Jas
Can't sleep.
잠이 안 와.

Kell2013
Too much coffee?
커피 너무 많이 마셨니?

 Jas
📎 sort of: 대충, 그냥, 좀 그래
Sort of.
좀

📎 coffee addict: 커피 중독자   Kell2013
No offense, but you're a coffee addict.
기분 나쁘게 하려는 건 아닌데, 너 커피 중독이야.

 Jas
Speak for yourself.
사돈 남 말 하시네.

📎 w/o: without의 약자   Kell2013
He he. But I just can't wake myself up w/o a morning coffee.
근데 모닝 커피 없인 깰 수가 없어.

Jas

♪ Same here: 마찬가지, 나도 그래

Same here.
나도 그래.

  Kell2013

♪ w: with의 약자

Speaking of which, r u ready for the presentation?
말이 나왔으니까 그런데, 프레젠테이션 준비는 다 했어?

 Jas

♪ born ready: 태어날 때부터 준비된, 준비 완료된

Of course. I was born ready.
당근. 200퍼센트 준비됐어.

Kell2013

Good.
잘됐다.

More to Talk!

 Oneself가 들어간 표현

Don't be so hard on yourself. 너무 자책하지 마.
Give yourself a little credit. 자신을 좀 칭찬해봐.
He started to talk to himself. 그는 혼잣말하기 시작했다.
Take a good look at yourself in the mirror. 거울 속의 네 모습 좀 잘 봐봐.
He prides himself on his good looks. 그는 자신의 외모에 자신감이 있다.

 039

He lives off ramen and soda.
걔는 라면과 탄산 음료로 살아.

 King_Michael
I'm too tired to meet tonight.
오늘 넘 피곤해서 못 만나겠다.

🔖 Spent: I spent를 줄인 표현

Me too. Spent all my energy at the gym.
나도, 체육관에서 에너지를 몽땅 썼어.

Tae

 겜폐남   🔖 ~suck: ~는 형편없다, 재수없다
What?! You guys suck.
뭐?! 니네 재수다.

 King_Michael
Sorry. It's just part of getting old.
미안. 나이 먹는 증상인 거여.

Ha! Yeah, I don't have energy like I used to.
하! 맞아. 나 예전같이 팔팔하지 않아.

Tae

 겜폐남
WOW You two sound like senior citizens...
Forget you guys! I'm gonna be up all night.
와. 니네 둘 노인네 같다... 집어치워 얘들아! 난 밤 꼬박 샐 거야.

King_Michael

Ohhh What's your secret?
오~ 비결이 뭔데?

♪ live off: ~에 의지해서 살다

Tae

He lives off ramen and soda.
쟨 라면이랑 탄산음료로 살아.

 겜폐남

Hahaha yeah. I call it the PC Room Diet.
하하하. 응. 난 PC방 다이어트라고 하는데.

 King_Michael   ♪ LMAO: Laughing My Ass Off (ass는 저속하므로 친한 친구끼리만 주로 쓰는 표현) 배꼽 빠지게 웃음

LMAO
빵터짐

 겜폐남

You should try it. I'm always energized. ;)
함 해봐. 난 항상 힘 받쥐~.

Tae

lol
ㅋㅋ

 에너지 충전과 관련된 표현

I stopped drinking energy drinks because they were giving me headaches. 난 두통이 생기기 때문에 에너지 드링크를 마시는 걸 중단했어.

Coffee doesn't agree with me. 커피가 안받아.

The doctor gave me a vitamin shot to help with the fatigue. 의사가 피로 회복을 돕는 비타민 주사를 놔줬어.

Too much caffeine will have you up all night. 카페인을 너무 섭취하면 밤을 꼬박 새게 될 거야.

ChitChat 040

What exactly is that?
정확히 그게 뭔데?

Kell2013
I invited my friends from the States to my place for dinner and I have no idea what to serve.
미국서 온 친구들을 집에 초대했는데 뭘 해줘야 할지 모르겠어.

🔖 **Give'em**: Give them을 줄인 표현   **Jas**
Give'em Bulgogi! It's always a hit w/ our foreign clients.
불고기 해줘! 우리 회사 외국인 고객들한테 항상 히트거든.

Kell2013   🔖 **vegan**: 엄격한 채식주의자
Can't. They're vegan. No meat.
안돼. 걔네 비건이거든. 고기는 안 먹어.

🔖 **vegetarian**: 채식주의자   **Jas**
Vegan? What exactly is that? Is it like being a vegetarian?
비건? 그게 정확히 뭔데? 채식주의자 같은 거야?

Kell2013
Like a vegetarian but stricter. No eggs, no cheese. No animal products of any sort.
채식주의자 같은 건데 좀 더 엄격해. 달걀, 치즈도 안 먹어. 동물성 식품은 몽땅 사절.

🔖 **kudos**: 칭찬, 찬사   **Jas**
Wow. Well kudos to them for their healthy lifestyle. Unfortunately it sounds like your menu options are pretty limited.
와우. 그 건강한 생활방식에는 박수를 보낸다만 유감스럽게도 할 만한 메뉴가 너무 제한되는 거 같다.

Kell2013

♪ soup broth: 국물 낸 것, 삶은 국물

Yeah. And everything I know how to make has seafood or eggs. :(They can't even eat soup broth made with anchovies.
응. 내가 아는 거라곤 해산물이나 달걀로 만드는 거뿐. ㅠㅠ 걔넨 멸치로 국물 낸 것도 안 먹어.

Jas

Guess you'll have to go with bibimbap. Minus the egg, of course.
비빔밥으로 해야겠네. 물론 달걀 빼고.

 Kell2013

And dessert?
그럼 디저트는?

Jas

Fresh fruit and tea? I bet they've never tried chamoe melon before.
신선한 과일과 차? 걔들 참외 먹어본 적 없을 거라고 확신해.

Kell2013

Good idea. I knew you'd be the person to ask.
좋은 생각. 너한테 물어봄 답 나올 줄 알았지.

More to Talk!

 건강식에 관한 표현

He is striving to eat more unprocessed foods for his health. 그는 건강을 위해 가공되지 않은 음식을 더 많이 섭취하려고 애쓰고 있어.

We switched to soy milk when we heard about growth hormones in regular milk. 일반 우유에 있는 성장 호르몬에 대해 듣고 나서 우린 두유로 바꿨어.

Choose the juice with the least amount of additives for your children.
자녀들을 위해 최소량의 첨가물이 든 주스를 선택하세요.

Many housewives purchase more expensive organic produce in hopes of preventing cancer. 암을 예방하기 위해 많은 주부들이 좀 더 비싼 유기농 식품을 구매한다.

I'm not sure what she's into.
그녀가 뭘 좋아하는지 잘 몰라.

Tae

I need your help.
도움이 필요한데.

겜폐남

With?
어떤?

Tae

I've got a date and I don't know where to take her. I'm not sure what she's into.
데이트가 있는데 어디로 그녈 데려갈지 모르겠어. 그녀가 뭘 좋아하는지 잘 몰라.

I'm not good with ~: ~에 약하다, 소질 없다

겜폐남

U know I'm not very good with the ladies.
내가 여자에 그리 강하지 못한 거 알잖아.

Tae

You gotta have some idea...
그래도 뭔가 아이디어가 있을 거 아냐...

Tae

Well I know what movie she wants to see. It's dinner I don't know what to do about.
어떤 영활 좋아하는지는 알아. 아이디어가 없는 건 바로 저녁식사야.

겜폐남

How about Italian? Girls love pasta. Or so I hear...
이탈리아 음식 어때? 여자들은 파스타 좋아해. 적어도 듣기로는...

Tae

Hmm...
음...

🎤 **~or something:** ~ 그런 거, 그딴 거

Otherwise something trendy. Like Indian or something.
아님 트렌디한 거. 인도음식 그딴 거.

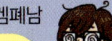 겜폐남

 Tae

You think she'd go for a Brazilian steakhouse? Unlimited meat.
브라질 스테이크집은 좋아할까? 고기 무제한인.

🎤 **She's not into it:** 그녀가 그것을 좋아하지 않는다.

 겜폐남

If she's not into it you can always date me ;)
그 여자가 그거 안 좋아하면 언제든 나랑 데이트 가능 ;)

 Tae

lol Ur not my type.
ㅋㅋ 넌 내 타입 아냐.

More to Talk!

 에스닉 푸드에 관한 표현

Most places serve frozen stuff but their sushi is all fresh. 대부분의 식당에서는 냉동한 것을 팔지만 그집 스시는 모두 신선해.

How about something exotic like Thai or Vietnamese? 태국이나 베트남 같은 이국적 음식 어때?

The curry at the Indian place near my office is amazing! 회사 근처에 있는 인도 식당의 카레는 끝내줘!

There are Chinese restaurants everywhere but it's hard to find an authentic one. 중국집은 어디에나 있지만 진짜 중국집은 찾기 어려워.

Instead of a big meal let's go for something light like wine and tapas. 푸짐한 음식을 먹기보다는 와인과 타파스 같은 가벼운 걸 먹자.

ChitChat 042

What should I eat to up my stamina?
스태미너 올리려면 뭘 먹어야 하지?

 동분서주

> Whew! It's steamy hot!!!
> 휴! 쩌죽겠네!!!

천사표

> Tell me about it.
> 그니까.

 동분서주

> What can I eat to up my stamina?
> 스태미너 올리려면 뭘 먹지?

♪ dunno: don't know의 인터넷 속어   천사표

> I dunno. Grilled eel?
> 몰라~. 장어구이?

동분서주 ♪ have a strong stomach: 비위가 강하다

Ewww! You sure have a strong stomach!
우웩! 너 진짜 비위 강하다!

♪ ~will do: ~면 된다, ~면 충분하다 천사표

Maybe samgyetang will do.
삼계탕 정도면 되겠지.

 동분서주 ♪ (Are you) up for ~: ~에 관심 있어?

Up for samgyetang, then?
그럼 삼계탕 먹으러 갈까?

천사표

Sure. The usual spot?
고럼. 늘 가던 거기?

 심한 더위와 관련된 표현

Hitting the movies is a good way to survive sizzling summer days. 여름 무더위에 살아남으려면 영화 관람이 제격이야.

I can't stand this hot, humid weather! 이런 덥고 습한 날씨 못 참겠어!

I'd rather it be freezing than scorching. I can always layer on more clothes. 타 죽느니 얼어 죽겠다. 옷이야 언제든 껴입음 되잖아.

I'm all sweaty. How do I stop my makeup from melting? 난 땀 범벅이야. 화장이 지워지는 걸 어떻게 막는다지?

Look. I'm sweating like a pig. 봐. 나 완전 땀 범벅이야.

ChitChat 043

I occasionally splurge on weekends. 가끔씩 주말마다 폭식해.

Kell2013
> You're looking thinner these days.
> 요즘 살 빠진 것 같은데.

> Am I?
> 내가?

Kell2013
> What's the big secret?
> 비결이 뭐야?

> The Half Food Diet.
> 반식 다이어트

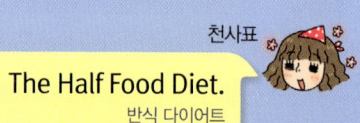

Kell2013
> Isn't that tough?
> 힘들지 않아?

> You know it.
> 당근.

Kell2013 🖉 OMG: Oh, my god를 줄인 말. 인터넷 속어. 어머나, 세상에
> OMG, how can U not be tempted?
> 어머나, 어떻게 유혹에 넘어가지 않을 수 있니?

🖉 splurge: 마구 먹다, 폭식하다, 팍팍 쓰다
> I occasionally splurge on weekends. HaHa.
> 가끔 주말마다 폭식해. 하하.

Kell2013
> LOL. Honestly, I would be tempted.
> ㅍㅎㅎ. 솔직히 나라면 유혹 받을 거 같은데.

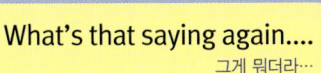

천사표
What's that saying again....
그게 뭐더라…

Kell2013
What?
뭐?

🎵 Hara ha chi bu: 뱃속을 80퍼센트만 채우라는 일본 속담

천사표
"Hara ha chi bu?"
"Hara ha chi bu?"던가?

Kell2013

🎵 yep: yes의 구어적 표현

Yep. "Eat until you feel 80% full."
응, 80퍼센트 정도 배가 찰 때까지 먹어라.

천사표
Eating less is good for you anyway.
어쨌든 소식이 몸에 좋으니까.

More to Talk!

다이어트 관련 표현

She's lost a ton of weight on the Lemon Detox Diet. 그녀는 레몬 디톡스 다이어트로 살을 엄청 뺐어.

The vocal trainee is on a protein only diet before his debut. 그 가수 연습생은 데뷔를 앞두고 황제 다이어트 중이다.

An unbalanced diet leads to malnutrition. 불균형한 식습관은 영양실조를 일으킬 수 있다.

The actor got hooked on diet pills. 그 영화배우는 다이어트 약에 빠졌다.

She's trying to get her figure back after childbirth. 그녀는 출산 후 몸매를 되찾기 위해 노력 중이다.

Diets are rarely successful in the long run because of the yo-yo effect. 다이어트는 요요 현상 때문에 장기적으로는 성공하기 힘들다.

ChitChat 044

The meat was dry and the veggies were all mushy.
고기는 푸석하고 야채는 완전 물렀어.

 Jas

The new Italian restaurant sucks!
새 이탈리안 레스토랑 완전 후졌어!

동분서주

The one in Jongno?
종로에 있는 거?

 Jas

Yes. I ordered the lunch special.
응. 런치 스페셜을 시켰거든.

동분서주

And?
근데?

 Jas

*veggies: vegetables의 약어

The meat was dry and the veggies were all mushy.
고기는 푸석하고 야채는 완전 물렀어.

동분서주

Sounds horrible.
듣기만 해도 심하네.

 Jas

And the servers are rude, too.
종업원들도 무례해.

🎵 déjà vu: 이미 본 느낌, 기시감   동분서주

Déjà vu.
데자뷰네.

 Jas

What?
뭐?

동분서주

That sounds just like the old restaurant there.
거기 있던 예전 레스토랑이랑 아주 똑같은 것 같아서.

 Jas

🎵 last: 지속되다

Hmmm.... That place didn't last that long.
거기 그리 오래 가지 않았지.

동분서주

Let's see if the new place gets any better.
혹시 나아질지 두고 보자.

More to Talk!

 맛있는 음식에 관한 표현

I have a craving for some scrumptious apple pie. 맛있는 애플 파이가 너무 먹고 싶다.

The seafood there was to die for. 거기 해산물은 둘이 먹다 하나 죽어도 모른다니까.

Thanks for the yummy cookies. 맛난 쿠키 고마워.

I'm drooling as I think of their naengmyeon. 그 냉면을 생각만 해도 군침이 돌아.

Let me show you how to make mouth-watering bibimbap. 군침 돌게 맛있는 비빔밥 만드는 방법을 알려주겠어.

Do they have any lo-cal options? 저칼로리 음식도 있대?

백조
> **Buffet tonight?**
> 오늘 밤에 뷔페 어때?

📎 Sry: sorry의 약어   천사표
> **Can't. Sry.**
> 못 가. 미안.

백조
> **Tomorrow?**
> 내일은?

천사표
> **I'm not sure...**
> 글쎄...

백조
> **You've been talking about going to this place for like two weeks!**
> 2주쯤 전부터 거기 가자고 내내 그러더니!

천사표
> **That was before I tried on my clothes from last summer...**
> 그건 작년에 입던 옷을 입어보기 전이지...

 백조

♪ Gotcha.: 알았어, 잡았다.

Gotcha. lol Italian then? That place by my house finally opened.
알아쓰. ㅋㅋㅋ 그면 이탈리아 음식 어때? 우리 집 근처 식당이 드뎌 개업했어.

♪ Depends = It depends. / lo-cal = low calories

Depends. Do they have any lo-cal options?
상황 봐서. 거기 저칼로리 음식도 있대?

 천사표

 백조

They probably have something. I'll call and find out.
뭔가 있을걸. 전화해서 알아볼게.

 천사표

Thanks! :D
고마워^^

More to Talk!

 영양 정보에 관한 표현

With this diet plan you have to count calories. 이 다이어트 계획으론 칼로리를 계산해야 해.

Eat foods low in saturated fat and cut down on sugar. 포화 지방산이 낮은 음식을 먹고 당분을 줄여.

They use artificial sweetener instead of sugar to save calories. 그들은 칼로리를 낮추기 위해 설탕 대신 인공 감미료를 사용해.

She lost 2 kilos by eating whole grains such as brown rice instead of white rice. 그녀는 흰쌀 대신 현미를 먹는 등 홀그레인(통곡물)을 섭취해서 2킬로를 감량했어.

Take a multivitamin to ensure you're getting the proper amount of vitamins and minerals. 적정량의 비타민과 미네랄 섭취를 확보하려면 멀티비타민을 복용해.

ChitChat 046

My stomach is growling.
뱃속에서 천둥 쳐.

동분서주
I'm so hungry!!!
넘 배고파!!!

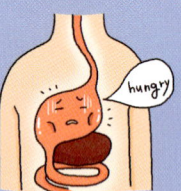

🔖 hr: hour의 약자
Kell2013
What??? U ate less than an hr ago.
헐??? 먹은 지 한 시간도 안 지났잖아.

동분서주
🔖 growling: 그르렁거리는
My stomach is growling.
뱃속에서 천둥 쳐.

Kell2013
Eat.
먹어.

동분서주
There's nothing to eat.
먹을 게 암것도 없어.

Kell2013
Come to think of it, didn't you start a diet?
생각해보니, 너 다이어트 중 아녔어?

동분서주
🔖 That' why ~.: 그래서 ~한 거야.
That's why I emptied my fridge.
그래서 냉장고 비운 거야.

Kell2013

I'm getting hungry.
나도 배고파진다.

동분서주 🔑 order in: (집으로) 시키다

Order in pizza.
피자 시켜.

Kell2013

Yeah, sounds good.
아, 걱 좋겠다.

동분서주

Ugh, I think I'm regaining my appetite!
아~~악. 다시 입맛이 도는 거 같아.

🔑 lost an appetite: 입맛을 잃다　Kell2013

Like you've ever lost it.
언젠 입맛 없었나.

동분서주　🔑 Can I come over (to your place)?: 너희 집에 가도 돼?

...can I come over? ....
가도 돼?

 허기와 갈증에 관련된 표현

I'm starving to death. 배고파 죽겠어.

He was extremely thirsty after working out. 그는 운동 후 몹시 목이 말랐다.

He's starved for love. 그는 사랑에 굶주려 있다.

Can sports drinks quench your thirst better than water? 스포츠 드링크가 갈증 해소에 물보다 더 나을까?

Cigarettes may help decrease your appetite. 담배는 입맛을 떨어뜨릴 수 있다.

Hunger is the best appetizer. 시장이 최고의 반찬이다.

What are you in the mood for?
뭐 먹고 싶어?

 동분서주

> So, when and where?
> 그럼, 언제 어디서 볼까?

 Kell2013

> 7ish?
> 7시쯤?

 동분서주

> K. Then where?
> ㅇㅋ. 그럼 어디서?

 Kell2013

> What are you in the mood for?
> 뭐 먹고 싶은데?

 동분서주

 light: (위에) 부담 없는, 가벼운

> Anything light. U?
> 너무 배부르지 않은 거면 상관없는데. 넌?

 Kell2013

🖊 Me 2.: Me too.의 인터넷 약어

> Me 2. I'm avoiding carbs these days.
> 나도. 요즘 탄수화물 자제하고 있어.

 동분서주

> Salad?
> 샐러드 어때?

🖊 You read my mind: 내 마음을 읽었네, 동의해, 좋아

 Kell2013

> You read my mind.
> 내 맘을 읽었네~

 동분서주

vegetarian: 채식주의자의

Know any good vegetarian restaurants?
채식 식당 좋은 데 알아?

Kell2013

I know one in Itaewon.
이태원에 하나 있어.

 동분서주

caught in traffic: 교통 체증에 걸린

Too far. Plus I don't wanna get caught in traffic.
너무 멀다. 글고 교통체증에 걸리기 싫어.

stick to: 끝까지 버티다

Kell2013

Good point. Let's stick to Gangnam.
알았쓰. 걍 강남에 있자.

 교통 체증에 관한 표현

There's nothing worse than being stuck in traffic. 교통 체증보다 끔찍한 건 없어.

Let's hit the road now and beat the rush hour traffic. 지금 출발해서 러시아워를 피하자.

I sat in traffic for more than 5 hours. 다섯 시간 이상 교통 체증에 시달렸어.

He prefers public transportation to avoid Monday morning rush hour. 그는 월요일 아침 러시아워를 피하기 위해 대중 교통을 선호한다.

It was bumper-to-bumper all the way to work. 회사 오는 길 내내 차가 꽉 막혔어.

CHAT 04 **119**

 048

You're hitting the gym pretty hard. 운동 꽤나 열심히 하는데.

King_Michael

🔖 Where u at?: Where are you at?을 줄인 표현(비문이지만 친한 사이에 사용)

> Where u at?
> 어디야?

Tae

> Why? Lol
> 왜? ㅋㅋ

 King_Michael

> Thought you were coming out for drinks?
> 한잔하러 올 줄 알았는데?

🔖 stop off: 잠깐 들르다 / tho: though의 약자

Tae

> At the gym now. I might stop off after tho.
> 짐 헬스장야. 이따 잠깐 들를까 해.

 King_Michael

🔖 hit the gym: 헬스장에 가다

> You're hitting the gym pretty hard these days.
> 요즘 운동 꽤나 열심히 하네.

🔖 bod: body의 약자, 몸 / Esp: especially의 약자, 특히

Tae

> Gotta work on my beach body. Lol Esp before my Jeju trip.
> 바닷가 갈 몸 만들어야 해서. ㅋㅋ 특히 제주여행 전에 말야.

King_Michael

Lol Yeah, I hear you. Been meaning to hit the gym myself.
ㅋㅋ. 응, 알것다. 나도 운동할 생각이었어.

🔍 come with: come with me를 줄인 말   Tae

You should come with.
같이 다니자.

King_Michael   🔍 cardio: cardiovascular의 약자, 심혈관의

You doing weight training or cardio?
근력운동? 아님 심폐운동?

🔍 Two birds with one stone.: 일석이조.   Tae

Both. Circuit training. Two birds with one stone.
둘 다. 순환 운동해. 일석이조야.

King_Michael

Nice.
좋네.

More to Talk!

 헬스에 관한 표현

I do 100 crunches every night to tone my abs. 난 복부 강화를 위해 밤마다 100개씩 복근 운동해.

Circuit training is the best way to burn fat and build muscle. 순환 운동은 지방을 연소하고 근육을 만드는 최선책이야.

He has been doing pushups to build up his upper arms, shoulders, and chest. 그는 팔뚝, 어깨, 흉부를 강화하기 위해 팔굽혀펴기를 하고 있어.

I heard doing squats is a great way to work on your lower body. 스쿼트를 하는 게 하체 단련을 위한 최적의 방법이라고 들었어.

Strength and endurance are important but a lot of people forget to work on flexibility as well. 힘과 끈기가 중요하긴 하지만 많은 사람들은 유연성도 길러야 하는 걸 잊고 있다.

ChitChat 049

My head is killing me.
머리 아파 죽겠어.

빈
Why aren't you answering your phone?
전화 왜 안받아?

백조
My head is killing me.
머리가 너무 아파서.

빈
What's wrong? You sick?
왜 그래? 아픈 거야?

백조
No. I'm okay.
아니. 괜찮아.

빈
I hear the flu is going around.
Need me to bring you some porridge or something?
독감이 돈다고 하던데. 죽이라도 가져다줘?

백조
It's not the flu. I just had a few too many last night.
독감 아냐. 어젯밤에 좀 과음했어.

빈
I thought you went home right after work?
퇴근 후에 바로 집에 간 줄 알았는데?

  백조
A friend called me out last minute.
친구가 막판에 전화했어.

 빈
Lol I'll be over in a few with some aspirin and ramen.
ㅋㅋ 좀 있다 아스피린이랑 라면 가져갈게.

백조
Ur the best.
니가 최고.

 빈
What would you do without me? :P
니가 나 없으면 어쩌겠니? (메롱)

More to Talk!

 가벼운 질병에 관한 표현

Just take some OTC drugs and you'll be better in no time. 일반 의약품 좀 복용하면 금방 나을 거야.

Be careful. I hear there's a stomach virus going around. 조심해. 장염이 유행한다더라.

I've come down with a cold and can't go to work. 난 감기에 걸려서 출근 못해.

It's just a little bug. I'll be fine. 그냥 감기 정도. 괜찮을 거야.

The doctor gave me a prescription for my sinus cold. 의사가 나의 코감기에 대해 처방전을 주었다.

 **050**

I'm quitting alcohol cold turkey!
나 술 딱 끊을 거야!

 Jas
> I'm dying.
> 죽을 것 같아.

 Kell2013
> Why?
> 왜

 Jas
> I drank too much last night.
> 어젯밤 과음했어.

 Kell2013
> Again? Another company dinner?
> 또? 또 회식?

 Jas

 soju bombs: 소주 폭탄주, 소폭
> Yes. We did soju bombs until late.
> 응. 늦게까지 소폭 마셨어.

 Kell2013
> You guys seem to get together every Friday night.
> 금요일 밤마다 회식하는 거 같은데.

 Jas
> I don't feel comfortable at office dinners, but it's hard to say no.
> 회식자리가 불편하지만 거절하긴 힘들어.

Kell2013
Totally agree with you.
완전 공감.

Jas
🖊 sleep the hangover off: 잠으로 숙취를 해결하다
I just wanna sleep this hangover off.
잠이나 푹 자서 숙취 좀 해결했으면.

Kell2013
Go for it. You need to prepare for the next one. :P
글케 해. 다음을 준비해야쥐. (메롱)

Jas
🖊 quit cold turkey: 딱 끊다
No! I'm quitting alcohol cold turkey!
아니! 술 딱 끊을 거야!

Kell2013
Easier said than done.
말이야 쉽지.

More to Talk!

 음주에 관한 표현

Let's have a toast! 건배하자.
I can't hold my liquor at all. 난 술 전혀 못해.
Do you know about the dog hair remedy? 숙취 해소법 알아?
What's the best way to avoid a hangover? 숙취를 피하는 가장 좋은 방법은 뭘까?
Drunk drivers often cause high speed collisions. 음주 운전자는 종종 과속 충돌 사고를 일으킨다.

I tripped texting and walking.
문자 치며 걷다가 발을 헛디뎠어.

동분서주
> **Bad news.**
> 나쁜 소식 있어.

 Jas
> **What?**
> 뭔데?

동분서주
> **I sprained my left ankle.**
> 왼쪽 발목 삐었어.

 Jas
> **How?**
> 어쩌다가?

동분서주
🎵 trip: 발을 헛디디다, 걸려 넘어지다
> **I tripped while texting and walking.**
> 문자 치면서 걷다가 헛디뎠어.

 Jas
> **HA! You were asking for it!**
> 하! 자업자득이었네!

동분서주
> **I'm in a half cast.**
> 반 깁스 하고 있어.

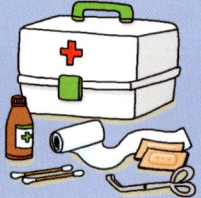

Jas
Is it very swollen?
많이 부었어?

 동분서주

n: and의 약어 / black and blue: (시퍼렇게) 멍든
Swollen n black and blue.
붓고 멍들었어.

Jas
So, no more high heels?
그럼 하이힐은 이제 굿바이야?

 동분서주
They're a no-no for now. At least my phone survived.
당분간 안돼. 그래도 폰은 살았어.

Jas
LOL Thank God!!!
ㅍㅎㅎ. 천만다행이네!!!

More to Talk!

 골절, 탈골에 관한 표현

I broke my leg. 다리 부러졌어.

I pulled a muscle in my leg. 인대가 늘어났어.

He dislocated his shoulder while snowboarding. 그는 스노보드를 타다가 어깨가 탈골됐다.

She twisted her ankle running. 그녀는 뛰다가 발목을 접질렸다.

I threw my back out. 난 허리를 삐끗했다.

ChitChat 052

My head feels foggy.
머리가 맑지 않아.

Kell2013

> How do you know if ur having a panic attack?
> 공황 장애가 있는지 스스로 어떻게 알아?

🎵 panic attack: 공황 장애

 천사표

> Umm..u have lots of stress n start freaking out? lol
> 음… 스트레스가 심하고 공포에 떨기 시작하나? ㅋㅋㅋ

Kell2013

> My head feels foggy and I can't stop sweating. I feel a little nauseous too.
> 머리가 맑지 않고 땀이 멈춰지지 않아. 구역질도 좀 나고.

 천사표

> What??! OMG
> 뭐? 맙소사.

Kell2013

> I tried calling someone but my words weren't coming out right.
> 누군가를 부르려고 했는데 입 밖으로 말이 나오질 않았어.

🎵 r u = are you

 천사표

> Where r u?
> 어디니?

Kell2013

> Home
> 집

 천사표

I'll be right there. I'll take you to the ER.
금방 간다. 응급실에 데려갈게.

 Kell2013
K
알았어

 천사표

Sit down and just try to breathe deep.
앉아서 심호흡 좀 해봐.

 Kell2013
K
응

천사표

Just hang on. I'm coming.
좀만 참아. 곧 갈게.

More to Talk!

 질병의 징후 관련 표현

If you're feeling dizzy, sit down. 어지러우면 앉아.

I am having trouble concentrating and I get upset very easily.
집중이 잘 안 되고 쉽게 화가 나.

He seems really forgetful these days. 그는 요즘 진짜 깜빡깜빡하는 것 같아.

I'm really tired and sluggish lately so I made a doctor's appointment.
요즘 정말 피곤하고 찌뿌듯해서 진찰 예약했어.

If it gets worse you should see a doctor immediately. 심해지면 즉시 병원 가야 해.

Worry can make you sick.
걱정하면 병 나.

 동분서주

> I heard about what happened with Kell2013. Is everything okay?
> Kell2013 얘기 들었어. 괜찮대?

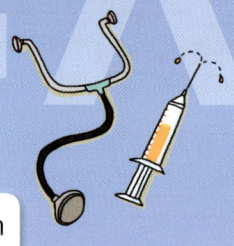

천사표

> Yeah. She's okay. We're at the hospital now.
> 응. 괜찮대. 우리 지금 병원이야.

 동분서주

> So what did they say is the problem?
> 문제가 뭐라던?

천사표

> The doctor said it's just stress.
> 의사가 그러는데 그냥 스트레스래.

 동분서주

> That's going to be hard for her, being a workaholic and all.
> 힘들겠네. 일 중독인데.

천사표

> They gave her a prescription and told her to take a few days off work.
> 처방전 주고 며칠 쉬랬어.

 동분서주

> How'd she take that?
> 걘 어떻게 받아들이던?

천사표

> Well, she started talking about who would take care of her projects.
> 자기 프로젝트를 누가 맡을지에 대해 얘기하기 시작하던데.

동분서주
OMG
어머!

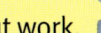 be worried about: ~에 대해 걱정하다  천사표
She is just really worried about work.
진짜 일 걱정뿐이라니까.

 동분서주
Jeez! This is really serious!
세상에! 거 정말 심각한데!

천사표
Yeah. :' (Her mom is going to come n take care of her for a few days.
그치. 걔네 엄마가 오셔서 며칠 보살펴 주신다더라.

 동분서주
That's a relief. So what they say is true... worry can make you sick.
다행이다. 그러니까 그 말이 맞네... 걱정 때문에 병 날 수도 있다더니.

 천사표
She'll be better after a few days. No better cure than rest and Mom's home cooking.
며칠 있으면 나을 거야. 휴식과 엄마가 해주는 집밥보다 나은 건 없으니까.

 동분서주
So true.
글타마다.

More to Talk!

 스트레스 해소에 관한 표현

Why don't you go away for the weekend to relieve some stress?
주말에 스트레스 줄일 겸 여행이라도 가는 게 어때?

I like to work off my stress by going for a run. 난 한바탕 달려서 스트레스를 날리는 걸 좋아해.

Whenever I get really stressed out I like to go hiking or do some other outdoor activity. 난 정말 스트레스 받을 때마다 하이킹 가거나 아웃도어 활동 하는 걸 좋아해.

The best way to beat stress is to spend time with friends. 스트레스를 이기는 최선책은 친구와 함께 시간을 보내는 거야.

I avoid stressful situations whenever possible. 나는 가능한 한 스트레스 받는 상황을 피해.

I'll keep my fingers crossed.
행운을 빈다.

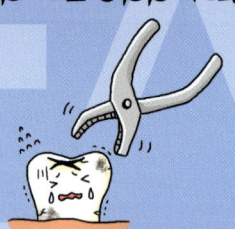

 Tae 🖉 big day: 대단한 날, 엄청난 날

> Today's the big day.
> 오늘은 엄청난 날이야.

Jas
> Oh?
> 응?

Tae
> I'm taking King_Michael to the dentist.
> King_Michael을 치과에 데려갈 거야.

Jas
> So what?
> 그게 뭐?

 Tae   🖉 apparently: ~해 보이는

> He hasn't gone in 10 years. Apparently he's deathly afraid.
> 걘 10년간 치괄 안 갔대. 무쟈게 겁나나 봐.

🖉 srsly: (seriously) 정말? 진짜야?   Jas
> Hahahaha Srsly?
> ㅎㅎㅎㅎ 정말?

 Tae 🖉 I kid you not.: 농담 아니야.

> I kid you not.
> 농담 아냐.

Jas
> What's the big deal?
> 왜 그런다냐?

Tae

 fill a cavity: 충치를 때우다

Some childhood fear... Had a dentist fill a cavity when he was young and it went all wrong.
어릴 때 느낀 공포 때문에… 어렸을 때 충치 때웠는데 완전 망쳤대.

Jas

Poor little guy :P Everything will be fine. lol
불쌍한 것 (메롱) 다 잘 될 거야.

Tae

I booked with the gentlest dentist in town. Just hope he actually shows and doesn't leave me hanging. Or worse...run out of the place screaming!
동네에서 제일 젠틀한 치과의사한테 예약했거든. 걔가 정말 오기만 바랄 뿐이야. 나 바람 맞지 않게. 아님 더 심하게… 비명 지르며 뛰쳐나가지 않길!

Jas

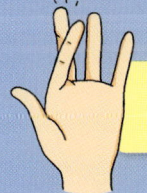

lol I'll keep my fingers crossed.
카캬. 행운을 빈다.

More to Talk!

 치위생에 관한 표현

My dentist always scolds me for not flossing. 내 치과의사는 치실 사용을 안 한다고 늘 야단을 쳐.

Brush your teeth after every meal and use a good mouthwash. 식사 후 매번 이를 닦고 좋은 구강 청정제를 사용해.

I'm thinking about getting my teeth professionally whitened. 난 전문 치아 미백을 받을 생각이야.

She had braces up until she was 17 and still has to wear a retainer at night. 그녀는 17세 때까지 교정기를 착용했고 지금도 밤에는 교정기를 껴야 한다.

They had to pull all of his wisdom teeth at once. 그들은 그의 사랑니를 한번에 몽땅 뽑아야 했어.

ChitChat 055

You'll be back to normal in no time.
곧 좋아질 거야.

Jas
I may have to postpone my trip to Hong Kong.
홍콩 여행 연기해야 할 거 같아.

Tae
Really? But you've been looking forward to it!
그래? 너 그 여행 기대했잖아!

Jas
🔖 take its toll: 나쁜 영향을 미치다
Yeah but I think all this work is starting to take its toll.
응. 근데 요즘 일이 너무 많아서 문제가 생긴 거 같아.

Tae
🔖 lenme= let me
Lemme guess... Your neck again?
가만 있자... 또 너 목이야?

Jas
You guessed it. I've tried everything but no luck.
맞아. 다 해봤는데 좋아지질 않아.

Tae
🔖 acupuncture: 침술 요법
What about acupuncture?
침을 맞아보는 건 어때?

Jas
Hmm... That's a thought! Know any Oriental clinics in the neighborhood?
음... 괜찮은 생각이네! 근처에 한의원 아는 데 있니?

Tae

In fact, I do! I'll text u the number.
사실, 있어! 번호 찍어줄게.

Jas

Great, thx.
잘됐다. 고마워.

Tae

My mom used to go there. Says it's great.
우리 엄마가 거기 다니셨거든. 좋다고 하셔.

Jas

Yeah? That's good to know.
그래? 잘됐네.

back to normal: 정상으로 돌아오다, 좋아지다

Tae

Give them a call. You'll be back to normal in no time.
전화해봐. 곧 좋아질 거야.

More to Talk!

전통 의학 관련 표현

My doctor gave me a mixture of herbs to take for weight loss. 의사가 나의 체중 감량을 위해 한약을 조제해 주었다.

Ginseng is good for people who have cold feet and hands. 인삼은 수족 냉증이 있는 사람에게 좋다.

When all the other treatments failed I turned to traditional medicine for a cure. 다른 모든 치료가 실패했을 때 치료를 위해 전통의학에 의존했다.

I prefer holistic forms of healing to modern Western medicine. 난 현대 서양 의학보다 홀리스틱한 치료 방법이 더 좋아.

Review

Words & Expressions CHAT 04

ChitChat 038 p 100
Speak for yourself.

No offense 악의는 없어, 기분 나쁘게 하려던 건 아니야
addict: 중독자
Speak for yourself. 사돈 남 말 하시네.
Same here. 나도 마찬가지야.
speaking of which 말이 나온 김에
born ready 완전히 준비된

ChitChat 039 p 102
He lives off ramen and soda.

senior citizen 노인
He lives off ramen and soda. 그는 라면과 탄산 음료로 살아.
fatigue 피로감

ChitChat 040 p 104
What exactly is that?

vegan 엄격한 채식주의자
What exactly is that? 그게 정확히 뭔데?
vegetarian 채식주의자
kudos 칭찬, 찬사
limited 제한된
seafood 해산물
unprocessed food 가공되지 않은 음식
additives 첨가물

ChitChat 041 p 106
I'm not sure what she's into.

(I'm) Not sure what she's into. 그녀가 뭘 좋아하는지 몰라.
trendy 트렌디한, 요즘 인기 있는
frozen 냉동의

ChitChat 042 p 108
What should I eat to up my stamina?

Tell me about it. 그러니까, 그렇다니까.
What should I eat to up my stamina? 스태미너 올리려면 뭘 먹지?
eel 장어
have a strong stomach 비위가 강하다
~ will do ~면 될 거야
usual spot 늘 가는 곳

ChitChat 043 p 110
I occasionally splurge on weekends.

tempted 유혹당하는
lose a ton of weight 살을 엄청 빼다
get hooked on ~에 빠지다
yo-yo effect 요요현상

CHAT 04

ChitChat 044   p 112
The meat was dry and the veggies were all mushy.

The meat was dry and the veggies were all mushy. 고기는 푸석하고 야채는 완전 물렀어.
veggies vegetables의 구어적 표현
place 식당, 가게, 집
have a craving for ~ ~가 땡긴다, 너무 먹고 싶다
scrumptious 아주 맛있는
yummy 맛있는

ChitChat 045   p 114
Do they have any lo-cal options?

(It) depends. 상황 봐서.
Do they have any lo-cal options? 저칼로리 음식도 있던?
count calories 칼로리를 계산하다
artificial sweetener 인공 감미료

ChitChat 046   p 116
My stomach is growling.

My stomach is growling. 뱃속에서 천둥 쳐.
come to think of it 생각해보니
order in (집으로) 시키다, 배달하다
appetite 입맛
quench 갈증을 해소하다
thirst 갈증
hunger 허기

ChitChat 047   p 118
What are you in the mood for?

What are you in the mood for? 뭐 먹고 싶니?
avoid 피하다
carbs(carbohydrates) 탄수화물
caught in traffic 교통 체증에 걸린
bumper-to-bumper 꽉 막혀서 오도가도 못하는

ChitChat 048   p 120
You're hitting the gym pretty hard.

You're hitting the gym pretty hard. 너 운동 꽤나 열심히 한다.
I hear you. 알겠다.
weight training 근력운동
cardio 심폐 운동
circuit training 순환 운동
do weight training 근력 운동을 하다
do cardio 심폐 운동을 하다

ChitChat 049   p 122
My head is killing me.

My head is killing me. 머리 아파 죽겠어.
flu 독감
go around 유행하다, 돌다
porridge 죽
last minute 막판에
OTC drugs(Over The Counter drugs) (처방전 없이 구매할 수 있는) 일반 의약품

CHAT 04

come down with a cold 감기에 걸리다

ChitChat 050   p 124
I'm quitting alcohol cold turkey!

hangover 숙취
sleep the hangover off 잠을 푹 자서 숙취를 해결하다
I'm quitting alcohol cold turkey. 나 술 딱 끊을 거야.
Easier said than done. 말이야 쉽지.
dog hair remedy 숙취 해소법

ChitChat 051   p 126
I tripped while texting and walking.

sprain 삐다
I tripped while texting and walking. 문자 치면서 걷다가 발을 헛디뎠어.
swollen 부은
black and blue 시퍼렇게 멍든
twist one's ankle 발목을 접지르다
throw one's back out 허리를 삐끗하다

ChitChat 052   p 128
My head feels foggy.

panic attack 공황장애
foggy 머리가 맑지 않은
My head feels foggy. 머리가 맑지 않아.
nauseous 구역질 나는

dizzy 어지러운

ChitChat 053   p 130
Worry can make you sick.

workaholic 일 중독자
prescription 처방전
take a few days off work 일을 며칠 쉬다
Worry can make you sick. 걱정하면 병 나.
relieve some stress 스트레스를 줄이다

ChitChat 054   p 132
I'll keep my fingers crossed.

deathly 심각하게, 굉장히
cavity 충치
leave someone hanging (결정을 하지 않아서) 누군가를 기다리게 만들다
I'll keep my fingers crossed. 행운을 빌게.

ChitChat 055   p 134
You'll be back to normal in no time.

take its toll 나쁜 영향을 미치다
acupuncture 침술 요법
Oriental clinic 한의원
You'll be back to normal in no time. 곧 좋아질 거야.
holistic forms of healing 신체뿐 아니라 정신적인 면까지 종합적으로 치료하는 방법

CHAT 05
Relationships
관계

- 056 She's driving me up the wall.
- 057 I couldn't believe my eyes!
- 058 Just don't screw this up.
- 059 You've got it all wrong.
- 060 He's creeping me out.
- 061 He's a total nightmare!
- 062 I'll make it up to you.
- 063 Things aren't the same anymore.
- 064 Let me get back to you later.
- 065 Your heart was in the right place.
- 066 We have a love-hate relationship.

ChitChat 056

She's driving me up the wall.
그녀 때문에 완전 돌겠어.

 겜페남

🎵 outta: out of의 구어 표현

Get me outta this house.
이 집에서 나 좀 꺼내줘.

🎵 prob: problem, 문제   빈

What's the prob now?
또 무슨 문제니?

 겜페남

🎵 drive someone up the wall: ~를 너무 화가 나게 만들다

It's my mom again. She's driving me up the wall.
또 우리 엄마야. 엄마 때문에 완전 돌겠어.

빈

She just wants you to get a job.
그저 직장 좀 구하라고 그러시는 거야.

 겜페남

🎵 hounding: 괴롭힘, 등쌀

Well it's not that easy!
And her hounding me certainly isn't helping.
글쎄, 그게 그리 쉽지 않다고! 날 그렇게 볶아대는 것도 전혀 도움이 되지 않고.

빈

She just needs to see that ur trying.
니가 노력하는 걸 보고 싶어하시는 것뿐이야.

겜폐남

I AM trying. Why can't she just trust me?
하고 있어. 왜 날 좀 믿어주지 못할까?

🖉 U'll: you'll의 인터넷 표현   빈

Keep searching. U'll find something soon.
계속 찾아봐. 곧 찾게 될 거야.

 겜폐남

Let's hope.
그러길 바라자.

🖉 in the meantime: 그 사이에, 그 동안에   빈

**In the meantime, just ignore her nagging.
It's just her worrying about you.**
그 동안엔, 엄마 잔소리는 그냥 무시해. 그냥 널 걱정하시는 것뿐야.

 More to Talk!

 짜증과 관련된 표현

Stop pestering me! 나 좀 들들 볶지 마!

My little brother is really annoying. 내 막내 남동생은 진짜 성가시게 해.

When I was younger the other kids teased me a lot. 어릴 때, 다른 애들이 나를 많이 놀려댔어.

It's really irritating when people don't use their headphones. 사람들이 헤드폰 안 쓸 때 진짜 짜증나.

It drives me nuts that my boyfriend drinks so much. 남자친구가 과음하는 건 나를 너무 짜증나게 한다.

ChitChat 057

I couldn't believe my eyes! 내 눈이 의심스럽더라!

 동분서주
You know Jean on the 5th floor?
5층에 있는 진 알지?

 Kell2013
That stuck up snob who never says hi to anybody first?
절대 먼저 인사 안 하는 그 건방진 여자?

 동분서주
Yes.
그래.

 Kell2013
What about her?
그 여자 뭐?

 동분서주
I just bumped into her in the elevator. And guess what?
응. 방금 엘리베이터에서 마주쳤거든. 근데 어땠게?

 Kell2013
What? Hurry up and spill.
어땠는데? 빨리 말해.

 동분서주
Like Hyun was in with me talking...
거기서 현과 얘기하고 있는데…

Kell2013

Oh, that hot shot lawyer Hyun?
아, 그 잘나가는 변호사 현?

 동분서주

♪ jump into conversation: 대화에 끼어들다

Yeah. And out of nowhere she jumped into our conversation.
응. 그 여자가 불쑥 대화에 끼어드는 거야.

♪ hit on ~: ~에게 수작을 걸다, 꼬리치다   Kell2013

Was she hitting on him?
꼬리치던?

 동분서주

More than that. She was all over him.
그 이상이야. 완전 들이대더라.

♪ He's out of her league.: 그가 여자에 비해 아깝다. 그가 그 여자에 비해 수준이 높다   Kell2013

Leave it alone. He's way out of her league anyway.
냅둬. 어차피 여자가 한참 기울어.

 동분서주

Still, I couldn't believe my eyes!
그래도, 내 눈이 의심스럽더라.

 성격과 관련된 표현

He's only shy with me. He's normally super outgoing. 그 남잔 나한테만 수줍어해. 보통은 완전 외향적인데.

She's a picky eater. 그녀는 편식이 심해.

He's narrow-minded and intolerant. 그는 옹졸하고 참을성이 없어.

I'm not a pushover. 난 호구가 아냐.

He's too stubborn to ever admit he's wrong. 그는 너무 고집이 세서 자신이 옳지 않다는 걸 인정하지 않는다.

Just don't screw this up.
이거 망치지 마.

 Tae

> I got you that interview.
> 니 면접 잡았어.

🎤 You rock!: 너 끝내준다, 너 짱이다.

> AWESOME! Thanks, man! You rock!
> 짱! 고마워, 친구! 너 진짜 짱이다! 겜페남

 Tae

🎤 ur: you're의 인터넷 표현(비문)

> I know. Haha. But it doesn't mean ur getting the job.
> 알아. 하하. 근데 그렇다고 취업이 된다는 건 아냐.

> I know. I know.
> 알아, 알지. 겜페남

 Tae

🎤 @ 4: at 4의 인터넷 표현. 네 시에 / Was=(It) was

> It's Monday @ 4.
> Was the only opening as Jas is leaving town that night.
> 월요일 네 시다. Jas가 그날 밤에 떠나기 때문에 그때밖에 안된대.

> Ok. Got it. Have a few things to do in the morning n I'm there.
> 오케이. 알겠어. 아침에 몇 가지 일 보고 거기 갈게. 겜페남

Tae

Just don't screw this up.
I don't wanna look stupid in front of Jas.
이거 망치지 마. Jas한테 우스워 보이고 싶지 않으니까.

겜폐남

Don't worry! I'm not going to mess up my only chance.
걱정 마! 한번뿐인 기회를 망칠 생각은 없어.

Tae

🔍 ya: you의 구어 표현

Alright, buddy. Best of luck to ya then.
좋아, 친구. 그럼 행운을 빈다.

🔍 rat race: 극심한 경쟁, 생존 경쟁

겜폐남

Thx. Hopefully I'll be part of the rat race next time we chat!
고마워. 모쪼록 담에 채팅할 땐 무한 경쟁 중이었음 하네!

More to Talk!

 실수 관련 표현

There isn't much you can do to make up for that kind of mistake. 그런 실수를 만회하기 위해 네가 할 수 있는 건 별로 없다.

I crashed and burned in my job interview. 취업 면접에서 퇴짜 맞았어.

Is it too late for me to fix the problem? 문제를 바로잡기엔 너무 늦은 건가?

He only said that to save face after that callous remark. 그는 그 모욕적인 말 때문에 체면 살리려고 그렇게 말한 것뿐이야.

You've got it all wrong.
너 완전 잘못 알고 있구나.

 Kell2013 🔖 hear through the grapevine: 정보를 듣다, 소문을 듣다

I heard through the grapevine that you're in town.
너 이 동네에 있다는 첩보가 있던데.

Jas

Yeah, but I'm leaving tomorrow.
맞아, 근데 내일 떠나.

 Kell2013

What?! How long have you been here?
뭐? 여기 얼마나 있었는데?

Jas

For 5 days now.
5일째.

 Kell2013

And you didn't think to message me?
근데 나한테 문자 할 생각은 안 했고?

 You've got it all wrong.: 너 완전 잘못 알고 있어.   Jas

But you've got it all wrong. I'm here to do interviews.
너 완전 잘못 알고 있구나. 나 여기 면접 때문에 온 거야.

 Kell2013   🔖 lunch or something: 점심 같은 거, 점심 그런 거

Still, we could have grabbed lunch or something.
그래도, 간단히 점심이라도 먹을 수 있잖아.

♪ hectic: 바쁜, 빡빡한   Jas

You know how hectic my schedule is.
내 스케줄이 얼마나 빡빡한지 알면서.

 Kell2013

Well how about tonight?
음. 오늘밤은 어때?

                                                          Jas

I'm meeting some game designers tonight.
오늘 밤엔 게임 디자이너들을 만나야 해.

 Kell2013

ALL night?
밤새?

♪ tonite = tonight   Jas

How about meeting just for a drink tonite?
자정에 만나 술 한잔할까?

 Kell2013   ♪ I'll take what I can get.: 그것밖에 (선택할 수) 없다면 그거라도 할게.

I'll take what I can get.
그것 밖에 안됨 그거라도 해야지 뭐.

 고집과 관련된 표현

Alright. If you insist, I'll take it. 좋아. 정 그렇다면, 받을게.

What should I do with this stubborn guy? 이 고집 센 남자를 어쩌면 좋지?

Like father like son. You two are so obstinate. 그 아버지에 그 아들. 당신들 둘 다 정말 고집이 세군요.

My puppy is very headstrong and hard to train. 우리 강아지는 고집 세고 훈련하기 힘들어.

Stop talking back to me! 말대꾸 그만 해!

ChitChat 060

He's creeping me out.
그 남자 때문에 소름 끼쳐.

빈
🔖 act weird: 이상하게 행동하다
겜폐남 is acting really weird.
겜폐남 행동이 좀 이상해.

동분서주
How so?
어떻게 이상한데?

빈
🔖 status: 상태 메시지
I dunno.. He just... Everywhere I go he's there. And whenever I update my status he is the first to comment. Always calling too.
몰라. 그냥… 내가 어딜 가든 걔가 있고. 내 상태 메시지를 업데이트할 때마다 걔가 제일 먼저 코멘트를 달아. 글고 맨날 전화하고.

🔖 What's the big deal?: 그게 뭐 어때서?
동분서주
What's the big deal? He's always online so he's the first to comment.
그게 대수야? 걘 늘 인터넷 하는 중이니까 코멘트도 젤 먼저 달겠지.

빈
🔖 or sumthin: (or something의 인터넷 표기) 뭐 그런 거, 그딴 거
He's creeping me out. U think he likes me or sumthin?
걔 때문에 소름 끼쳐. 걔가 나 좋아하거나 그런 거 같니?

🔖 paranoid: 피해망상증의 / awkward: 어색한
동분서주
Stop being paranoid! He's just a little awkward is all.
망상 좀 하지 마! 그냥 걔가 좀 어색해서 그런 것뿐야.

빈

🎵 *drink* coffee: drink 앞뒤의 별표(*)는 강조를 나타냄.

He keeps asking me about different coffee blends. I'm pretty sure he doesn't even *drink* coffee.
걔가 계속 각종 커피 블렌드에 대해 물어보는 거야. 커피는 전혀 마시지도 않는 걸로 아는데.

동분서주

U really think there's somethin else going on?
너 진짜 뭔가 딴 게 있다고 생각하는 거야?

 빈

Not sure. Maybe it's nothing.
글쎄. 암것도 아닐 수도 있겠지.

🎵 bout =about / tell: 구분하다, 분간하다

동분서주

How bout I come by ur shop next time he's there? I'll be able to tell if he's being weird.
담에 걔가 거기 간 날 내가 너네 커피샵에 들르면 어때? 이상하게 구는지 내가 보면 알 것 같아.

 빈

🎵 (I) was just about to ~ : 방금 막 ~하려고 했어.

Was just about to suggest that!
막 그렇게 말하려고 했어!

 More to Talk!

 남다름과 관련된 표현

He is acting kind of peculiar. 걔 좀 유별나게 구네.

Everyone around me is acting really odd. 내 주변에 있는 사람들은 다 좀 특이해.

It's unusual that my boss would call at that hour. 우리 사장님이 그 시간에 전화하는 건 흔한 일이 아니야.

People are saying a lot of strange things. 사람들이 별의 별 이상한 얘기를 하고 있어.

Something funny is going on but I have no idea what! 뭔가 일이 묘하게 돌아가는 거 같은데 그게 뭔지 모르겠어!

 **061**

He's a total nightmare!
그 남자 완전 악몽이야!

빈
Hey. U there? I think I'm gonna scream...
안녕. 거기 있지? 비명 지르고 싶어.

Kell2013
What's up?
무슨 일야?

빈
Ugh. Where do I even begin...
어디서부터 얘기한다지…

Kell2013
Uh-oh. Is this about your interview?
어~, 인터뷰 때문인 거야?

빈
I never told you? They gave the job to someone else!
얘기 안했나? 그 자리에 딴 사람을 뽑았어.

Kell2013
I'm so sorry to hear that.
정말 안됐다.

빈

🎵 He's a micromanager.: 그는 사소한 것까지 모두 간섭해.

Yeah... And the guy they gave it to acts like a drill sergeant. He is always yelling, rude to customers, and is a micromanager.
어... 글구 그 자리에 뽑힌 남잔 꼭 훈련 조교 같아. 맨날 고함치고, 고객들한테 무례하고, 사소한 것까지 다~ 간섭해.

Kell2013

He sounds like a nightmare.
악몽 같네.

빈

He's a total nightmare! I'm already looking for another job.
그 남자 완전 악몽이야! 나 벌써 딴 데 알아보는 중이야.

Kell2013

Good idea. It's probably time to move on anyway.
좋은 생각. 갈 길 찾아 갈 때가 된 것 같다.

More to Talk!

 유감을 나타내는 표현

You poor thing! 불쌍한 것!
That's too bad. 정말 안됐다.
That's a shame. 안됐디.
I can't believe it. 믿어지지 않네.
No way! 그럴 수가!

ChitChat 062

I'll make it up to you.
보상할게.

Jas
It's 6. Where are you?
6시야. 어디 있어?

Kell2013
Running 30 minutes late.
30분 늦을 거야.

Jas
Not again!
또야!

🎵 make it up to: ~에게 만회하다, 보상하다
Kell2013
I'll make it up to you!
보상할게.

Jas
I'm getting pretty tired of always waiting for you.
항상 기다리려니 심히 지겹다.

🎵 a ton of traffic: 엄청난 교통량
Kell2013
Don't be mad, there's a ton of traffic.
화내지 마, 길이 너무 막혀.

Jas
🎵 put up with ~: ~을 참다
I don't know why I put up with you anymore. >:O
내가 왜 더 이상 널 참아야 하는지 모르겠어.

🔍 **come clean**: 자백하다, 자수하다

Kell2013

I'll come clean. I'm running late because I had to change.
자수할게. 사실은 옷 갈아 입어야 해서 늦은 거야.

 Jas

Change? Why?
갈아입어? 왜?

Kell2013

I didn't want to go out wearing my work clothes.
근무할 때 입는 옷 입고 나가기 싫었어.

 Jas

I should just go home!
그냥 집에 갈까 보다!

🔍 **overdramatic**: 과대하게 반응하는

Kell2013

**Don't be so overdramatic.
I said I would make it up to you somehow.**
너무 과잉반응 하지 마. 어떻게든 보상해 준다니까.

 Jas

Well, you had better make it good!
제대로 보상하는 게 좋을걸!

 More to Talk!

 화와 관련된 표현

Don't be angry at me. I'll explain. 화내지 마. 해명할게.
Stop pissing me off! 나 성질 건드리지 마!
He started getting on my nerves. 그는 내 신경을 긁기 시작했다.
He has a bad temper. 그는 못된 성미를 가지고 있다.
My brother is hot-tempered. 우리 오빠는 다혈질이야.

ChitChat 063

Things aren't the same anymore.
더 이상 옛날 같지 않거든.

겜폐남
U busy?
바빠?

겜폐남
Hello?
여보셔?

빈
Where r the guys these days?
요즘 다들 어딨니?

겜폐남
I dunno. Don't see much of them. Things aren't the same anymore.
몰러. 많이 못 봐. 더 이상 예전같지 않거든.

Y's that = Why is that

빈
Y's that?
왜 그래?

겜폐남
Not sure. I think they are avoiding each other. Or me. Who knows?
글쎄. 서로 피하는 거 같아. 아님 나를(피하나). 알 게 뭐야?

빈
That's too bad.
유감인데.

겜폐남

🔊 wanna go = Do you want to go / place: 가게, 식당

So, wanna go to that noodle place I was telling you about?
내가 말했던 국수집 갈래?

빈

Umm... hold on a sec.
음. 잠시만.

빈

Yeah. Ok. Let's go.
응. 오케이. 가자.

 겜폐남

Great. I'll pick you up in 10.
쪼아. 10분 후에 픽업 갈게.

🔊 btw = by the way

빈

동분서주 is coming too btw.
그건 그렇고 동분서주도 갈 거야.

 겜폐남

K.
ㅇㅋ

More to Talk!

 모른다고 말할 때 쓰는 표현

Who knows? 누가 알아?
How should I know? 내가 알아?
I wouldn't know. 모르지.
No idea. 몰라.
I haven't the slightest idea. 전혀 몰라.
Beats me! 몰래!

CHAT 05 **155**

Let me get back to you later.
좀 있다 알려줄게.

Kell2013
> Got plans for tonight?
> 오늘 밤에 약속 있어?

♪ hubby = husband 남편

천사표
> I think I'm gonna stay in with my hubby.
> 남편이랑 집에 있을까 해.

Kell2013
> Just bring him out too.
> 그냥 남편도 같이 나와.

천사표
> Why? What's going on?
> 왜? 무슨 일인데?

Kell2013
> There's a new restaurant opening. It should be fun.
> 새로운 레스토랑이 오픈한다는데. 재밌을 거 같아.

천사표
> My husband is being really lazy today.
> 남편이 오늘 진짜 게으른 거 있지.

Kell2013
That's not news. He's always lazy.
어제오늘 일도 아니잖아. 언제나 게으른데 뭐.

 천사표
He's just been sitting around all day, I don't even think he showered.
하루 종일 빈둥거리고 샤워도 안 한 거 같아.

 Kell2013
🔗 TMI = Too Much Information 그 정도까진 알고 싶지 않다
Gross!!! TMI.
드러워!!! 알고 싶지 않아!!!

 천사표
Wait. Let me get back to you later.
기다려. 좀 있다 알려줄게.

 Kell2013
Don't be too late, I need to make reservations!
너무 늦진 마. 예약해야 하니깐!

More to Talk!

 개인 위생에 관한 표현

Wash your hands as soon as you get home. 집에 오자마자 손 씻어.

Cleansing wipes are convenient for taking makeup off. 클렌징 티슈는 화장 지울 때 편리해.

Using deodorant is a must in the summer. 여름엔 탈취제 사용이 필수야.

Wearing damp socks is bad for you. You may get athlete's foot. 젖은 양말 신고 있는 건 좋지 않아. 무좀에 걸릴 수 있거든.

Stop picking your nose! 코 좀 그만 후벼!

ChitChat

Your heart was in the right place. 의도는 좋았지.

백조
I feel so lousy.
기분 넘 더럽다.

♪ Boo: 자기야. (친한 사이에서 부르는 애칭)

동분서주
What's the matter, Boo?
왜 그래, 자갸?

백조
Where do I even start? Ugh. So apparently that guy I went on a few dates w/ is King_Michael's friend.
어디서부터 얘기해야 하나? 윽. 몇 번 만난 남잔 얘긴데, King_Michael 친구였더라고.

동분서주
No way! How'd you find out?
세상에! 어쩌다가?

♪ turn white: 얼굴이 하얘지다, 깜짝 놀라다

백조
We ran into him on our way to dinner!
When he saw us together his face turned white.
저녁 먹으러 오는 길에 마주쳤어! 우리가 같이 있는 걸 보더니 얼굴이 하얗게 질리더라.

동분서주
Oh my god. Did you say anything?
저런. 무슨 말이라도 했어?

백조

♪ n: and의 인터넷 약어

I said hi and he pretended like he was really busy n left. I felt so bad I called him later that night to say sorry for everything.
내가 인사했더니 그 남자가 진짜 바쁜 척하고는 가버렸어. 기분 넘 안 좋아서 그날 밤 나중에 전화해서 어쨌든 미안하다고 했지.

 동분서주

You didn't have to do that. You didn't do anything wrong!
뭐하러 그랬어. 니가 뭘 잘못한 것도 아닌데!

 백조

♪ smooth things over: 좋게 넘어가다, 원만하게 해결하다

He freaked out on me for calling. I just wanted to apologize and maybe smooth things over.
전화했다고 버럭하더라. 사과하고 좋게 넘어가려고 했을 뿐인데.

♪ rly = really 정말, 진짜

동분서주

Your heart was in the right place but u rly shouldn't have called him.
의도는 좋았지만 진짜 전화할 필요까진 없었어.

 백조

♪ now I know: 이젠 알겠어, 그니까

Now I know.
그니까.

More to Talk!

 우연한 만남과 관련된 표현

What a coincidence it is to see you here! 여기서 널 보다니 대단한 우연인데!
He just appeared out of nowhere. 그는 불현듯 나타났다.
I turned around and guess who was there! 돌아봤더니 거기 누가 있었게!
I bumped into her on my way to work. 회사 가는 길에 그녀와 우연히 마주쳤다.
I looked up and saw my old roommate standing in front of me. 올려다보니까 앞에 옛날 룸메이트가 서 있더라.

ChitChat 066

We have a love-hate relationship.
우린 애증의 관계야.

동분서주
> 빈 is so annoying!
> 빈 땜에 정말 짜증나!

🎵 get along: 잘 지내다, 사이 좋게 지내다

 백조
> Uh-oh are you two fighting again? Why can't you just get along?!
> 너네 둘 또 싸우니? 그냥 사이 좋게 지낼 수 없어?

동분서주
> Ask her. She's the reason we fight.
> 걔한테 물어봐. 걔 때문에 싸우는 거니까.

 백조
> Yeah yeah. You say that now but last week you two were doing everything together. Are you going to cancel on the Busan trip?
> 그래 그래. 그건 지금 하는 소리고 지난 주만 해도 둘이 줄창 붙어다녔잖아. 부산으로 여행가는 거 취소할 거야?

동분서주
> Me? Why should I?
> 나? 내가 왜?

🎵 bicker: 말다툼하다, 논쟁하다

 백조
> Well if you two are fighting then one of you should. I'm not listening to bickering the entire weekend.
> 너네 둘이 싸우고 있다면, 둘 중 하나는 그래야지. 주말 내내 말다툼하는 거 들어줄 생각은 없으니까.

동분서주
It's not that bad... And if anyone cancels it should be her!
그 정도까진 아니야... 글구 누군가 취소한다면 걔여야 해!

unbearable: 참을 수 없는

백조
When you two fight it's unbearable for the rest of us.
너네 둘이 싸우면 나머지 우리가 너무 힘들어.

동분서주
We'll be fine I promise. More than fine actually! We're going to have so much fun!
괜찮을 거라고 약속할게. 사실 괜찮은 거 이상일 거야! 정말 재밌을 거야!

백조
So now you're okay with her?
그럼 걔랑 괜찮은 거지?

동분서주
What can I say? We have a love-hate relationship.
어쩌겠니? 우린 애증 관계인데.

More to Talk!

 싸움과 관련된 표현

Is it really worth getting upset over? 그게 정말 기분 나빠할 만한 가치가 있나?

I hate when people argue over such trivial things. 그런 사소한 일들로 사람들이 말다툼하는 게 싫어.

As mad as you are it's still not okay to raise your voice. 아무리 화가 났어도 목소리를 높이는 것은 좋지 않아.

The lady in the drama got so mad she threw a glass of water in her boyfriend's face. 그 드라마에 나오는 여자는 너무 화가 나서 자기 남친의 얼굴에 잔에 있던 물을 쏟아버렸어.

He started cursing at me so I just hung up. 그가 욕설을 해대길래 그냥 끊어버렸어.

Review — Words & Expressions　　CHAT 05

ChitChat 056　　p 140
She's driving me up the wall.

Get me out. 나 좀 꺼내 줘.
prob. problem의 줄인 표현
What's the prob? 뭐가 문제니?
She's driving me up the wall. 그녀 때문에 완전 돌겠어.
hounding 등쌀, 괴롭힘
helping 도움이 되는
Let's hope. 그러길 바라자.
in the meantime 한편으로, 그 사이에
nagging 잔소리
ignore one's nagging ~의 잔소리를 무시하다
pester 들들 볶다
Stop pestering me. 나 좀 들들 볶지마.
annoying 짜증나게 하는
tease 놀리다
drive someone nuts ~를 미치게 만든다

ChitChat 057　　p 142
I couldn't believe my eyes!

stuck up snob 시건방진 사람
bump into 마주치다
hot-shot 거물급의, 잘나가는
out of nowhere 불쑥, 갑자기
jump into one's conversation ~의 대화에 끼어들다
hit on ~ ~에게 수작을 걸다
More than that. 그 이상이야.
all over ~ ~에게 애정공세를 퍼붓는

out of one's league ~에 비해 수준이 높은
I couldn't believe my eyes. 내 눈이 의심스럽더라.
super outgoing 완전 외향적인
picky eater 음식에 까탈스러운 사람
narrow-minded 옹졸한
intolerant 참을성이 없는
pushover 만만한 사람, 쉬운 일, 호구
stubborn 고집 센
admit 인정하다

ChitChat 058　　p 144
Just don't screw this up.

You rock! 너 끝내준다!
the only opening 유일하게 남은 빈 시간
opening 빈 시간
Got it! 알겠어!
Just don't screw this up. 이거 망치지 마.
mess up 망치다
buddy 친구
hopefully 모쪼록
rat race 극심한 생존 경쟁
make up for ~ ~를 만회하다
crash and burn 퇴짜 맞다
fix the problem 문제를 바로 잡다
save face 체면을 살리다
callous remark 모욕적인 언사

ChitChat 059　　p 146
You've got it all wrong.

hear through the grapevine 소문을 듣다

CHAT 05

message 문자메시지(를 보내다)
You've got it all wrong. 너 완전 잘못 알고 있구나.
grab lunch 간단히 점심 먹다
hectic 바쁜
I'll take what I can get. 그거밖에 (선택할 수) 없다면 그거라도.
if you insist 정 그렇다면
Like father like son. 그 아버지에 그 아들.
obstinate 고집 센
headstrong 고집대로 하는
Stop talking back to me. 말대꾸 그만 해.

ChitChat 061   p 150
He's a total nightmare!

drill sergeant 훈련 조교
yell 고함치다
rude 무례한
micromanager 사소한 것까지 모두 간섭하는 사람
He's a total nightmare. 그 남자 완전 악몽이야.
You poor thing! 불쌍한 것, 가여운 것
That's a shame! 안됐다!
No way! 그럴 수가!

ChitChat 060   p 148
He's creeping me out.

weird 이상한
act weird 이상하게 행동하다
status 상태 메시지
update one's status 상태 메시지를 업데이트하다
What's the big deal? 그게 대수야?
creep someone out ~를 소름끼치게 하다, 섬뜩하게 하다
He's creeping me out. 그 남자 때문에 소름 끼쳐.
paranoid 피해망상증의
Stop being paranoid! 과대 망상 좀 하지마!
awkward 어색한
be about to~ 막 ~하려던 참이다
eccentricity 괴상함, 남다름
peculiar 유별난
act odd 별나게 행동하다

ChitChat 062   p 152
I'll make it up to you.

Not again! 또야!
I'll make it up to you. 만회할게.
get tired of ~ ~때문에 지겹다
a ton of traffic 엄청난 교통량
put up with 참다
come clean 자백하다, 자수하다
run late 늦다
work clothes 작업 복, 근무할 때 입는 옷
overdramatic 과하게 반응하는
somehow 어떻게 해서든
Stop pissing me off! 성질 나게 하지 마.
get on one's nerves 의 신경을 긁다
have a bad temper 성미가 못되다
hot-tempered 다혈질의

CHAT 05

ChitChat 063 — p 154
Things aren't the same anymore.

Things aren't the same anymore. 더 이상 옛날 같지 않아.
avoid each other 서로를 피하다
Who knows? 알 게 뭐니?
noodle place 국수 집, 국수 가게
hold a sec 잠시만
pick someone up ~를 데리러 가다, 픽업하다

ChitChat 064 — p 156
Let me get back to you later.

stay in with someone ~와 함께 집에 머물러 있다.
hubby 남편
bring someone out ~를 데리고 나오다
sit around 빈둥거리다
gross 끔찍한, 징그러운
Let me get back to you later. 좀 있다 알려줄게.
cleansing wipes 클렌징 티슈
take makeup off 화장을 지우다
deodorant 탈취제
damp 축축한
athlete's foot 무좀
pick one's nose 코를 후비다

ChitChat 065 — p 158
Your heart was in the right place.

lousy 기분 더러운, 끔찍한
boo 자기, 자기야
on one's way to ~ ~로 가는 길에
turn white 얼굴이 하얘지다, 깜짝 놀라다
pretend ~한 척하다
freak out 버럭하다, 기겁하다
smooth ~over 를 원만하게 해결하다, 좋게 넘어가다
Your heart was in the right place. 의도는 좋았지.
Now I know. 이제 알겠어.
coincidence 우연의 일치

ChitChat 066 — p 160
We have a love-hate relationship.

get along 잘 지내다, 사이좋게 지내다
cancel 취소하다
Why should I? 내가 왜?
bicker 말다툼하다
unbearable 참을 수 없는
We have a love-hate relationship. 우린 애증 관계야.
argue 논쟁하다
trivial 사소한
raise one's voice 언성을 높이다
curse 욕설을 하다

CHAT 06

Tech
기술

- 067 My contract is up.
- 068 Just give it a go!
- 069 I'm having trouble figuring this thing out.
- 070 This is my last resort.
- 071 It's gonna blow your mind!
- 072 It's revolutionized my life!
- 073 It keeps turning off.
- 074 I shrank my entire wardrobe.
- 075 Who can keep track of all these accessories?!

 **067**

My contract is up.
내 약정이 만료됐어.

 빈

> Need your opinion about a phone.
> 폰에 대해 니 의견이 필요해.

겜페남

> You've come to the right guy! What's up?
> 제대로 찾았네. 뭔일이야?

 빈

> Which is better, Apple or Samsung?
> 애플과 삼성 중 어느 쪽이 더 나아?

🎵 depend on ~: ~에 따라 다르다, ~에 달려 있다   겜페남

> It depends on the phone really. Why?
> 폰에 따라 다르지. 왜?

 빈

> My contract is up. I'm not sure if I should switch providers either.
> 약정이 만료됐거든. 통신사를 변경해야 할지도 잘 몰겠고.

🎵 (phone) service plan: 전화 요금제   겜페남

> I'm pretty happy with mine. How much data comes with your service plan? 난 내꺼에 꽤 만족해. 니 요금제엔 데이터가 얼마나 제공되니?

빈
2GB. And I get 500 minutes.
2기가야. 글구 500분 무료.

겜폐남
For how much?
얼마에?

빈
90,000 won.
9만 원.

🎣 rip off: 바가지
겜폐남
What a rip off!
완전 바가지네!

빈
Ah... I thought it might be.
U think you could come cell phone shopping with me?
아, 그럴 거 같더라. 나랑 휴대폰 사러 같이 갈 수 있을까?

📱 cell phone: 휴대폰

겜폐남
It'd be my pleasure.
물론이지.

More to Talk!

 휴대폰 관련 표현

I lost the charger and have to get a new one. 충전기를 잃어버려서 새 거 사야 해.

You can get a prepaid phone at the airport when you arrive. 도착하면 공항에서 선불 전화를 살 수 있어.

ABC Mobile is now offering family plans. ABC 모바일은 이제 가족 요금제를 제공하고 있다.

They have rollover minutes so it's not a big deal if they use too much airtime. 잔여분이 이월되기 때문에 휴대폰을 많이 써도 별 문제가 되지 않는다.

My phone doesn't have a good signal. 내 전화는 수신이 잘 되지 않아.

CHAT 06 **167**

ChitChat 068

Just give it a go! 걍 덤벼봐!

Kell2013
Help!!! I have Trojan viruses on my laptop.
도와줘!!! 노트북에 트로이 목마 바이러스 걸린 거 같아.

🎵 get rid of ~: ~을 없애다

동분서주
Then get rid of them. U know how, right?
제거해. 방법 알지?

Kell2013
Told you I know nothing about computers.
컴퓨터 하나도 모른다고 했잖아.

동분서주
Just give it a go.
걍 덤벼봐.

Kell2013 🎵 okey-doke: ok의 변형, 알았어, okey-dokey
Okey-doke.
알써.

Kell2013
I'm ready now. How?
이제 준비 됐어. 어떡해?

동분서주
Delete the entire browsing history first.
먼저 브라우징 기록을 전부 삭제해.

Kell2013 🎵 I'm on it: 그렇게 할게, 한다니까
Um... I'm on it.
그렇게 할게.

동분서주

If you can't remove it all, follow the file location and delete the "temporary internet files".
없앨 수 없으면, 파일 위치를 찾아서 "임시 인터넷 파일"을 전부 삭제해.

 Kell2013

Ugh. It won't work.
어억~~~. 안 되는데.

installation: 설치

동분서주

Then you're gonna have to use an installation disk to reinstall Windows.
그럼 윈도우를 재설치하기 위해 윈도우 설치 디스크를 사용해야 할 거야.

 Kell2013

Ahhhh, it's getting more complicated.
으으. 점점 더 복잡해지네.

동분서주

Don't forget to back up your data before formatting your computer.
컴퓨터 포맷하기 전에 데이터 백업하는 거 잊지 마.

 Kell2013

I won't.
잊지 않을게.

More to Talk!

 컴퓨터 관련 표현 1

My nephew is computer savvy. 내 조카는 해박한 컴퓨터 지식을 갖고 있어.

Computers age fast. 컴퓨터는 금세 구식이 된다.

How do I hook this phone up to my computer? 이 전화기를 어떻게 내 컴퓨터에 연결시킨다지?

Have you ever had your computer turn off w/o warning? 혹시 컴퓨터가 경고 없이 꺼진 적 있니?

Tell me how I can install this software on my computer. 내 컴퓨터에 이 소프트웨어 설치하는 방법을 알려줘.

ChitChat 069

I'm having trouble figuring this thing out. 이 문제를 해결하느라 애먹고 있어.

빈

🎤 have trouble -ing: ~하느라 고생하다

I'm having trouble figuring this thing out.
이 문제를 해결하느라 애먹고 있어.

Which thing?
어느 거?

백조

빈

🎤 tech-savvy: 전문적인 기술을 갖춘, 테크에 능한

This tablet I bought for my aunt. Are you tech-savvy?
이모 드리려고 산 이 태블릿. 너 기술적인 거 잘 아니?

Somewhat. What's the problem?
조금. 문제가 뭔데?

백조

빈

🎤 n stuff: and stuff의 약자, 그런 거, 같은 거

I wanna get it set up with programs n stuff before I give it to her but not sure how to download'em.
드리기 전에 프로그램 같은 거 세팅하고 싶은데 어떻게 다운받는지 모르겠어.

You need an account.
계정이 필요해.

백조

빈

Ah, do I have to use my credit card?
아, 신용카드 사용해야 하니?

백조

I think if you want any paid apps. You should also set it up with your info instead.
유료 앱을 받으려면 그렇지. 글구 니 정보로 대신해서 세팅해야 해.

빈

Why's that?
왜 그런데?

🎵 ruin the surprise: 깜짝 놀라게 해줄 계획(선물, 파티 등)을 망치다

백조

She might get an email about the account and it'd ruin the surprise.
계정에 관해 너네 이모한테 이메일이 갈 수도 있는데 그럼 깜짝 선물을 망치게 되잖아.

빈

🎵 thinkin': thinking

OH good thinkin'. What kind of apps do you think a 50-year-old would like?
오, 좋은 생각. 50살 된 사람이 좋아할 게 어떤 앱일까?

🎵 You know: 알잖아, 뭐

백조

Hmm. Something for photos, another for organization, maybe one for recipes. You know, the basics.
사진, 일정정리, 요리법 같은 거. 기본적인 거지.

컴퓨터 관련 표현 2

I installed a few plugins on my browser to make my workflow more efficient. 좀 더 능률적인 작업의 흐름을 위해 브라우저에 몇 가지 플러그인을 설치했어.

You're running the outdated version. 넌 구버전을 사용하고 있어.

If you enter the password incorrectly 3 times it locks. 비번을 세 번 잘못 입력하면 잠겨버려.

You need to install the updates first. 업데이트된 항목을 먼저 설치해야 해.

When you download a torrent you should scan it for viruses. 토렌트를 다운할 때 바이러스 방지를 위해 스캔해야 해.

This is my last resort.
이게 최후 수단이야.

겜폐남

🔍 YT: You there의 약자, 거기 있니?

Hey, YT?
안녕, 거기 있어?

빈

Can't talk. Having a life crisis!
얘기 못해. 인생의 위기야!

겜폐남

What's wrong?
왜 그래?

빈

My hard drive just crashed and I can't retrieve my files.
하드 드라이브가 나갔는데 파일 복구가 안돼.

겜폐남

Didn't you back them up?
백업 안했어?

빈

NO, that's why it's a life crisis!
아니. 그니까 인생의 위기라는 거야!

🔖 **This is my last resort.**: 기댈 곳이라곤 이것뿐이다. 이게 최선책이다.

I'm about to go to the service center. This is my last resort!
서비스 센터에 가야겠어. 이게 최선책이야.

 겜폐남

Doesn't your computer automatically back up on a cloud?
네 컴퓨터는 자동으로 클라우드에 백업되지 않니?

 빈

Cloud?
클라우드라고?

 겜폐남

Yeah, your files should be there.
응, 네 파일들이 거기 있을 수 있어.

 빈

How do I get it from a cloud?
클라우드에서 어떻게 가져오는데?

 겜폐남   🔖 **ring you**: 너한테 전화하다

I'll ring you and explain!
전화해서 설명해줄게!

 컴퓨터 관련 표현 3

Help me with formatting my computer. 컴퓨터 포맷하는 것 좀 도와줘.
What now? My computer froze. 또 뭐야? 내 컴퓨터 먹통됐어.
My computer is running slower than usual. 컴퓨디가 평상시보다 느려.
Your computer screen seems blurry. 네 컴퓨터 모니터 좀 흐린 거 같아.
Help! My computer monitor's blinking on and off. 도와줘! 내 컴퓨터 모니터가 깜빡여.

ChitChat 071

It's gonna blow your mind!
완전 감동일걸!

King_Michael
Guess who's the new owner of a brand new convertible.
신상 오픈카의 새 주인이 누구게?

Tae
I think I can guess...
알 것 같은데…

King_Michael
It's a Beamer too.
게다가 BMW야.

Tae
Nice.
좋은데.

King_Michael
📎 fully loaded: 모든 옵션을 갖추고 있는
It's fully loaded. And it has a hard top that opens and closes automatically.
옵션 빵빵하지. 게다가 자동 개폐되는 하드 탑이 있어.

Tae
Sweet.
멋지다.

King_Michael

🔖 **top of the line**: 최고급의, 최신식의

The sound system is top of the line, too. You'll see this weekend. It's gonna blow your mind!
사운드 시스템도 최고급이야. 이번 주말에 보게 될 거야. 완전 감동일걸!

Tae

I bet it will. Having money must be nice, bro.
분명 그럴 거야. 돈 있는 거 확실히 좋은 거군, 친구.

 King_Michael

It sure is.
정말 그래.

Tae

Lol
ㅋㅋ

 King_Michael

Don't worry, I'll be sure to take you around town in it.
걱정 마. 꼭 태워서 시내 구경시켜줄게.

Tae

You'd better!
고레야지!

 **More to Talk!**

 운전과 관련된 표현

Before getting your license you have to attend a driving school. 면허 따기 전에 운전 학원에 다녀야 한다.

Always check your tires before a long road trip. 긴 도로여행 전에 항상 타이어를 체크해야 한다.

My car is in the shop till Saturday. 내 차는 토요일까지 카센터에 있어.

Children must always buckle their safety belts and babies must ride in car seats. 아이들은 반드시 안전 벨트를 매야 하고 아기들은 카 시트를 타야 한다.

Don't be a backseat driver! 운전 중에 잔소리 좀 그만해!

CHAT 06 **175**

It's revolutionized my life!
그게 내 인생을 확 바꿔버렸지!

 천사표

Our new kimchi refrigerator finally came!
우리 새 김치 냉장고가 드디어 왔어!

📎 Congrats: Congratulations의 약어 Kell2013

Congrats! How do you like it?
축! 어때?

 천사표

It's SO convenient. Now all the other food doesn't smell like kimchi.
너~무 편해. 이제 딴 음식에서 김치 냄새 날 일은 없어.

Kell2013

Lol
ㅋㅋ

 천사표

I'm so psyched!!!!!!!
완전 신나!!!!!

Kell2013

Haha Calm down! It's just a fridge.
하하, 진정해! 그래봤자 냉장고지.

 천사표

> JUST a fridge? It's revolutionized my life! Think I might order a blender next.
> "그래봤자" 냉장고라구? 그게 내 인생을 확 바꿔버렸어! 담엔 블렌더를 주문할까 생각중야.

Kell2013

> So how about you invite me over for dinner so I can see it?
> 저녁식사 초대해서 나한테 좀 보여줌 어때?

 천사표

🔖 be about to ~: 막 ~하려 하다

> OMG I was just about to! How's Friday for you?
> 에고. 방금 그러려고 했는데! 금욜 어때?

🔖 hectic: 바쁜, 정신 없이 빡빡한   Kell2013

> Things are really hectic at the office. The weekend is better. Sunday?
> 사무실에서 딥따 바쁘거든. 주말이 나을 듯. 일욜?

 친사표

> Sunday it is!
> 일욜이닷!

More to Talk!

 김치에 관한 표현

There are several varieties but the most common type is cabbage kimchi. 종류가 몇 가지 있지만 가장 흔한 것은 배추 김치이다.

Fermented foods are good for health. 발효 음식은 건강에 좋다.

I love the spicy, pungent taste of cooked kimchi. 난 강하고 톡 쏘는 익은 김치를 좋아한다.

This kimchi recipe has been passed down from generation to generation. 이 김치 만드는 법은 대대로 이어져 내려왔다.

It's delicious but inconvenient to store. 맛있긴 하지만 저장하기 불편하다.

ChitChat 073

It keeps turning off.
그게 계속 꺼져.

King_Michael

I'm going to die from heat exhaustion.
일사병으로 쓰러지겠어.

🔍 heat exhaustion: 일사병

 겜폐남

LOL What's going on?
ㅋㅋ 무슨 일이야?

King_Michael

My air conditioner. It keeps turning off.
에어컨. 계속 꺼져.

겜폐남

Call the manufacturer. They'll send someone out to fix it.
제조업체에 전화해. 수리할 사람 보내줄 거야.

King_Michael

I did. It's too old to be covered under warranty.
했어. 너무 오래돼서 보증이 안 된대.

겜폐남

Did they say about how much they would charge?
비용이 얼마나 들 거라고 얘기하던?

King_Michael

🔍 ain't: be/have 동사의 부정형으로 쓰임(비문)

They said it ain't gonna be cheap and they can't send anyone for a week.
수리 비용이 싸진 않을 거고, 이번 주엔 사람을 보낼 수 없대.

♪ repairman: 수리공, 기술자

 겜페남

Why not try calling a repairman? Jas was pretty happy with the one he used.
기술자한테 전화해보지 그래? Jas가 써본 사람이 꽤 괜찮았다던데.

 King_Michael

I don't feel like spending the money.
거기에 돈 쓰기가 싫거든.

 겜페남

It's going to be one hot summer for you!
무쟈게 더운 여름이 될 텐데.

 King_Michael

Yeah. Maybe I'll just buy a new one...
응. 걍 하나 새로 살까 봐.

 겜페남

So much for not wanting to spend the money.
언젠 돈 쓰기 싫다며.

 King_Michael

What can I say, I prefer new electronics!
어쩌라고, 난 새 가전이 좋은걸!

A/S에 관한 표현

You should take it to the service center for repair. 그거 수리 받으려면 서비스 센터에 가져가야 해.

The repairs cost more than the actual product! 수리비가 실제 물건값보다 더 나왔어.

Water damage is not covered under the warranty. 침수로 인한 손상은 품질 보증에 포함되지 않아.

Insurance for small electronics seems like a waste of money. 소형 가전제품을 보험에 드는 것은 돈 낭비 같아.

Can you recommend a good repair shop? 괜찮은 수리점 추천해줄 수 있어?

I shrank my entire wardrobe.
옷이 몽땅 줄어버렸어.

동분서주

My washing machine is a piece of garbage.
내 세탁기 완전 쓰레기야.

백조

LOL
ㅍㅎㅎ

동분서주

🎵 shrink: 줄이다, 줄다

It's not funny. All my clothes are ruined!
하나도 안 웃겨. 옷이 몽땅 망가졌어.

🎵 or something: 그런 거

백조

Did the washer rust or something?
세탁조가 녹슬거나 그런 거 아냐?

동분서주

🎵 malfunction: 오작동되다, 오작동

No. I clearly hit "normal wash" and it malfunctioned and somehow used hot water.
아냐. 분명 "일반 세탁"을 눌렀는데 오작동돼서 어쩐 일인지 온수가 나왔어.

🎵 Oh man.: 이런, 저런(낭패, 놀라움을 나타냄).

백조

Oh man.
아, 저런.

동분서주

I shrank my entire wardrobe.
내 옷이 몽땅 줄어버렸어!

백조

So what are you going to do?
그럼 어쩔 건데?

동분서주

🎵 I feel like suing.: 고소하고 싶은 기분이야.

I don't know but I feel like suing the manufacturer!
잘 몰겠는데 제조업체를 고소하고 싶어!

백조

That sounds rational. :P
말 되네. 메롱~

동분서주

🎵 roomie: roommate의 약어, 룸메이트

Until I figure this out I guess I'll have to wear my roomie's clothes. >:/
이걸 해결할 때까진 내 룸메이트의 옷을 입어야 할 거 같아.

More to Talk!

가전 제품에 관한 표현

The icemaker on the fridge is broken. 냉장고의 제빙기가 고장났다.

Hot water won't come out of the water cooler unless it's plugged in.
전원에 연결하지 않으면 음료수냉각기에서 온수가 나오지 않아.

The vacuum still functions but has poor suction. 진공청소기가 여전히 작동은 되는데 흡입력이 약해.

Don't forget to clean the filter every few weeks! 몇 주마다 필터 청소하는 거 잊지 마.

You need a dehumidifier in the summer and a humidifier in the winter.
여름엔 제습기가 필요하고 겨울엔 가습기가 필요해.

I wish our house had a dishwasher. 우리집에 식기 세척기가 있었으면 좋겠다.

ChitChat 075

Who can keep track of all these accessories?!
누가 이런 부속품들을 일일이 챙길 수 있겠니?

빈

Ack! I think I left my charger at your place.
악! 너네 집에 내 충전기 두고 왔나 봐.

동분서주

Really? I didn't see it.
정말? 못봤는데.

빈

It's got to be there somewhere.
My headphones aren't in my bag either!!
거기 어딘가에 있을 거야. 헤드폰도 가방에 없어!

🔖 lying around: 아무렇게나 놓여 있다, 여기저기 흩어져 있다

동분서주

I definitely didn't see any headphones lying around.
헤드폰 굴러다니는 거 절대 못봤어.

빈

Oh well. My battery is too low. I can't listen to music anyway.
아 그래. 뭐 어차피 배터리가 떨어져가서 음악도 못 들으니까.

동분서주

I just bought new earphones myself. I'm always losing them.
나도 요전에 이어폰 새로 샀는데, 나도 맨날 잃어버리거든.

🔖 keep track of: 추적하다, 파악하다

빈

I know! Who can keep track of all these accessories?!
그니깨! 이런 부속품들을 누가 일일이 챙길 수 있겠니?!

동분서주

Just don't replace yours with such expensive ones this time.
이번엔 그렇게 너무 비싼 걸로 바꾸지 마.

빈

I'll be sure not to. Can you keep looking just in case they're there?
안 그럴려구. 혹시 거기 있을지도 모르니까 계속 좀 찾아봐줄래?

동분서주

Will do. What color were they again?
그럴게. 무슨 색이라고?

빈

Hot pink.
핫핑크.

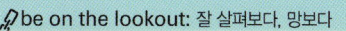 be on the lookout: 잘 살펴보다, 망보다

동분서주

 **I'll be on the lookout!**
잘 살펴볼게.

빈

Thx.
고마워.

 전원에 관련된 표현

Use my phone, it's fully charged. 내 폰 써. 완충됐어.

Use a power strip instead of plugging directly into the wall to save power. 전원을 아끼려면 벽에 직접 꽂지 말고 멀티탭을 사용해.

This room doesn't have enough electric sockets. 이 방은 전원 소켓이 충분치 않아.

Ask the waiter if they can charge your phone while we eat. 우리가 먹는 사이에 폰 충전이 되는지 웨이터한테 물어봐.

My battery is running low. I'll have to switch it. 배터리가 떨어져서 바꿔야 해.

Can you charge it with this USB cable? 그걸 이 USB 케이블로 충전할 수 있니?

More to Talk!

Review — Words & Expressions — CHAT 06

ChitChat 067 p 166
My contract is up.

come to the right guy 제대로 찾아오다
My contract is up. 내 약정이 만료됐어.
switch 변경하다, 바꾸다
(service) provider 통신사
service plan 약정, 전화 요금제
What a rip off. 완전 바가지네
cell phone 휴대폰
charger 충전기
prepaid phone 선불 전화기
family plans 가족 요금제
rollover 이월
have a good signal 수신이 잘 되다, 잘 터지다

ChitChat 068 p 168
Just give it a go!

Trojan virus 트로이 목마 바이러스
Just give it a go! 그냥 해봐!
Okey-doke OK의 변형된 표현
browsing history 브라우징 히스토리
I'm on it. 그러고 있어, 하고 있어.
temporary 임시의
It won't work. 안돼, 안되는데.
installation 설치
complicated 복잡한
format 포맷
computer savvy 컴퓨터 전문가인, 컴퓨터에 해박한 지식을 가지고 있는

hook up 연결시키다
warning 경고

ChitChat 069 p 170
I'm having trouble figuring this thing out.

figure out 알아내다, 해결하다
I'm having trouble figuring this thing out.
이 문제를 해결하느라 고생하고 있어.
tech savvy 전문적인 기술을 갖춘
somewhat 다소, 약간
account 계정
paid apps 유료 앱
ruin the surprise 깜짝 놀래줄 계획을 망치다
Good thinking. 좋은 생각이야.
recipe 요리법
basics 기본적인 것
outdated version 구버전
incorrectly 부정확하게
scan 스캔하다

ChitChat 070 p 172
This is my last resort.

life crisis 인생의 위기
hard drive 하드 드라이브
crash 망가지다
retrieve 회수하다, 검색하다
This is my last resort. 이게 최후의 수단이야.

automatically 자동적으로
I'll ring you and explain. 전화해서 설명해줄게.
It froze up. 먹통됐어.
blurry 흐린
blinking 깜빡거리는

ChitChat 071   p 174
It's gonna blow your mind!

convertible 오픈 카, 컨버터블
Beamer BMW
fully loaded 모든 옵션을 갖추고 있는
Sweet! 멋지다!
top of the line 최고급의
It's gonna blow your mind. 완전 감동일걸.
take someone around ~를 데리고 다니다
shop 카센터
buckle 매다
safety belt 안전벨트
Don't be a backseat driver. 운전 중에 잔 소리 좀 그만 해.

ChitChat 072   p 176
It's revolutionized my life!

kimchi refrigerator 김치 냉장고
psyched 신나는
I'm so psyched! 완전 신나!
fridge 냉장고
revolutionize 개혁하다, 완전히 바꿔 놓다

It's revolutionized my life. 내 인생을 확 바꿔 버렸지.
cabbage 배추
fermented food 발효 음식
spicy 양념이 강한
pungent 톡 쏘는
recipe 요리법
pass down 대대로 이어지다
from generation to generation 대대로
store 저장하다

ChitChat 073   p 178
It keeps turning off.

heat exhaustion 일사병
die from heat exhaustion 일사병으로 죽다
air conditioner 에어컨
It keeps turning off. 그게 계속 꺼져
manufacturer 제조업체
warranty 품질 보증
repairman 수리공
electronics 가전제품, 전자제품
water damage 수해
a waste of money 돈 낭비
repair shop 수리 센터

ChitChat 074   p 180
I shrank my entire wardrobe.

shrink 줄다, 줄이다

CHAT 06

I shrank my entire wardrobe. 옷이 몽땅 줄어 버렸어.
washer 세탁조
rust 녹슬다
or something. 그런 거
normal wash 일반 세탁
malfunction 오작동(하다)
sue 고소하다
I feel like suing. 고소하고 싶어.
figure out 알아내다
ice maker 제빙기
water cooler 냉각기
vacuum 진공 청소기
suction 흡입
clean the filter 필터 청소하다
Dehumidifier 제습기
humidifier 가습기
dish washer 식기 세척기

ChitChat 075   p 182

Who can keep track of all these accessories?!

charger 충전기
lie around 아무렇게나 놓여 있다
keep track of ~ ~를 추적하다, 파악하다
Who can keep track of all these accessories? 누가 이런 부속품들을 일일이 챙길 수 있겠니?
replace 교체하다, 바꾸다
be on the lookout 망보다
fully charged 100퍼센트 충전된
electric sockets 전원 소켓

CHAT 07

Leisure Activities
여가 활동

- 076 Bored out of my mind.
- 077 I haven't gone anywhere in ages.
- 078 He's an athletic freak.
- 079 I'm drawn to baking classes.
- 080 Let's get together more often.
- 081 It was a waste of time.
- 082 No wonder you're so good at English!
- 083 That's my show!
- 084 Just the thought of it makes me cringe.
- 085 I feel like an entirely new person.
- 086 Where is your sense of adventure?

Bored out of my mind.
지루해서 미치겠어.

백조
What are you doing now?
뭐해?

빈
Nothing. Bored out of my mind.
멍때려. 지루해서 미치겠어.

백조
Me too! I'm sick of sitting in my room every weekend!
나두! 주말마다 방콕하기 지겨워!

빈
Let's go somewhere! Wanna?
어디 가자! 그럴래?

백조
Right now?
지금 당장?

빈
Why not? How about a picnic by the river? We can order chicken!
안돼? 강가로 피크닉 어때? 치킨 시키고!

 백조

I like the sound of that! Do you want to ride bikes?
맘에 드네! 자전거 탈래?

빈

Of course! I think my little brother left a kite here too.
고럼! 내 남동생이 연도 여기 둔 거 같아.

 백조

 **Wow! I haven't flown a kite since I was a kid!**
와우! 어렸을 때 이후로 연 날려 본 적 없는데!

빈

It's gonna be great!
딥따 재밌을 듯!

 백조

Grab your sunglasses and meet me there!
선글라스 챙기고 거기서 보자!

More to Talk!

 여가활동에 관한 표현

All the children gathered around to build a sand castle. 애들 전부가 모래성을 쌓기 위해 모여들었어.

If you don't like swimming you can always work on your tan. 수영이 싫다면 언제든 썬탠할 수 있어.

There's nothing better than going to the ballpark with friends. 친구들과 야구장에 가는 거보다 좋은 건 없어.

Let's go to the soccer field and kick a ball around. 축구장에 가서 공이나 차자.

If you go there in early spring you can catch the Cherry Blossom Festival. 이른 봄에 거기 가면 벚꽃 축제를 볼 수 있어.

We went on a double date to Everland. 우리는 에버랜드로 쌍쌍 데이트 갔어.

ChitChat 077

I haven't gone anywhere in ages.
어딘가로 떠나본 지가 언젠지 몰라.

동분서주
> R U going anywhere during the summer holidays?
> 여름 휴가 때 어디 가니?

Kell2013
🎵 I can't afford it.: 그럴 여유가 없다
> You know I can't afford it. U?
> 그럴 여유 없는 거 알잖아. 넌?

동분서주 🎵 sis: sister의 약자
> Visiting my sis in LA.
> LA에 있는 언니를 방문하려고.

🎵 BTW: by the way의 약자. 그건 그렇고   Kell2013
> Nice. BTW, what's she doing there?
> 좋겠다. 근데 너네 언니는 거기서 뭐해?

동분서주 🎵 home making: 가사 일, 집안 일
> Homemaking.
> 집안 일.

Kell2013
> I see.
> 글쿤.

동분서주 🎵 make time: 시간 내다, 짬을 내다
> Make some time n come with me.
> 짬 내서 같이 가자.

Kell2013
> U know what my work is like.
> 내 일 어떤지 알잖아.

동분서주

🔍 **work 24/7**: 밤낮을 가리지 않고, 24시간 일주일 내내

This is crazy. You can't work 24/7!!!
말도 안돼. 항상 일만 할 순 없어!!!

Kell2013

It's bad timing. I just got another project.
시기가 나빠. 또 다른 프로젝트를 맡게 됐거든.

 동분서주

Alright.
알것수.

Kell2013

Maybe some other time.
담에 기회 봐서.

 동분서주

Freelancing doesn't mean you're free.
그려. 자유업의 자유가 그 자유는 아니지.

Kell2013

You tell me. I haven't gone anywhere in ages.
그니까. 어딘가 떠나본 지가 언젠지 몰라.

More to Talk!

연락하기와 관련된 표현

We'll see. 봐서.
Maybe next time. 담에나.
See you in 20. 20분 있다가 보자.
Can I take a rain check? 담에 할 수 있을까?
Call me. Don't be a stranger. 전화해. 연락 끊지 말고.

He's an athletic freak.
그 남잔 운동에 미쳐 있어.

Kell2013
How was your date?
데이트 어땠어?

동분서주
Don't even start.
얘기 꺼내지도 마.

Kell2013
What's wrong?
왜 그래?

🔖 talk nonsense: 헛소리하다   동분서주
He kept talking nonsense...
말도 안 되는 얘길 계속하고…

Kell2013
So he's humorous.
그니깐 유머 있단 얘기네.

동분서주
All he was talking was about giving workout advice.
얘기한 거라곤 운동에 대한 조언뿐이었다니까.

Kell2013 🔖 well-informed: 박식한, 해박한
So he was well-informed.
그니깐 해박하다는 얘기고.

🔖 workout freak: 운동광, 운동에 집착하는 사람   동분서주
And the worst part is he was an athletic freak.
근데 최악은 그 남자가 운동에 미쳐 있단 거야.

Kell2013

🔖 well-built: 체격 좋은. 몸 좋은

Oh, he must be well-built!!!
몸 좋겠네!!!

동분서주

STOP!!! It's annoying.
그만!!! 짜증 나.

Kell2013

lol. Sooooory!
ㅋㅋ. 미이이이이안!

🔖 rub it in: 염장 지르다. 불 난 집에 부채질하다

동분서주

You don't have to rub it in.
불 난 집에 부채질할 건 없잖아.

Kell2013

I said sorry.
미안하다고.

동분서주

...

Kell2013

Go for a beer? It's on me.
맥주나 한잔? 내가 쏠게.

 운동과 관련된 표현 1

There's nothing like running on the treadmill. 러닝 머신에서 뛰는 것만 한 게 없다.
Use the correct footwear to protect your joints. 관절을 보호하려면 맞는 신발을 신어.
Yeah!!!! It was time well-spent in the gym. 야~~, 체육관에서 시간 잘 보냈다.
Your trainer will help you set up the workout routine. 운동 절차를 정하는 데 트레이너가 도움이 될 거야.
Stay hydrated during your workout. 운동할 때는 물을 계속 마셔.
Most guys dream of having 6-pack abs. 대부분의 남자들은 초콜릿 복근을 꿈꾼다.

ChitChat 079

I'm drawn to baking classes.
베이킹 수업에 관심이 가네.

 Kell2013

Congrats! Now you're a certified barista.
추카추카! 인제 공인된 바리스타네!

Thx. But I have mixed feelings.
고마워. 근데 복잡한 기분이야.

 Kell2013

Haven't you decided on what to do next?
담에 뭘 할지 결정 못했어?

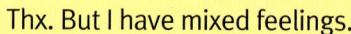
🎤 nah: 아니 (=no)

Nah.
응.

 Kell2013

I thought you wanted to open a coffee place.
커피숍을 하고 싶어하는 줄 알았는데.

That was my original plan, but I've changed my mind.
그게 원래 계획이었는데. 맘이 달라졌어.

 Kell2013

🎤 build up expertise: 전문 기술(지식) 쌓다

So, you want to build up coffee expertise working as a barista?
그럼 바리스타로 일하면서 커피에 관한 전문 기술을 기르게?

🔎 (I) can't picture ~: ~를 상상할 수 없다

천사표

Can't picture myself working for someone else.
딴사람 밑에서 일하는 게 상상이 안돼.

 Kell2013

What are you up to doing, then?
그럼 뭘 하려고?

천사표

Well, running a bakery?
베이커리 사장?

 Kell2013

…

천사표

I'm drawn to baking classes lately.
요즘 베이킹 수업에 관심이 가더라.

 Kell2013

Uhmmm, at least you have some plans. Good.
음… 그래도 계획은 있네. 좋아.

More to Talk!

 직장에 관련된 표현

He is a temp. 그는 임시직이다.

Flexible working hours can't be guaranteed for 9-to-5ers. 일반 정규직원들은 유연한 근무 시간을 보장 받을 수 없다.

Thanks to the five day work week system, he can have more quality time with his family. 주 5일 근무체제 덕분에 그는 가족들과 좀 더 많은 양질의 시간을 갖게 되었다.

All temp workers long to be regular workers someday. 모든 비정규직들은 언젠가 정규직이 되길 바란다.

CDF Mart hired 1,000 seasonal workers. CDF 마트는 한시적 인력을 1,000명 고용했다.

Let's get together more often.
우리 좀 더 자주 뭉치자.

 동분서주
Hey guys!
안녕, 얘들아.

 빈
Hi there.
안녕!

 동분서주
♪ blast: 너무 재미있는, 신나는
That was a blast!!!
너무 재밌었어!!

  백조
Same here. Fat burning n stress relief through working out...
마찬가지. 운동으로 지방 연소와 스트레스 해소까지...

 동분서주
It's like killing two birds with one stone.
일석이조 같아.

  백조
♪ muscular: 근육의
And all the muscular guys in the gym...
글구 체육관에 있던 근육남들…

빈

🎵 positive outlet: 긍정적인 (도움이 되는) 배출구, 발산 수단

lol I know! Exercise sure is a positive outlet!
ㅋㅋ 그니깨! 운동은 분명 긍정적인 배출구야!

🎵 on a regular basis: 규칙적으로, 정기적으로

 백조

lol Why don't we do this on a regular basis?
ㅋㅋ 우리 이거 규칙적으로 하는 게 어때?

 동분서주

Good idea.
좋은 생각.

빈

Let's get together more often.
우리 좀 더 자주 뭉치자.

백조

🎵 fit and healthy: 튼튼하고 건강한

Working out is necessary to keep fit and healthy anyway.
튼튼하고 건강을 유지하려면 어쨌든 운동은 필수니까.

🎵 Hear: 옳소!

빈

Hear! Hear!
옳소! 옳소!

More to Talk!

 운동과 관련된 표현 2

Let's hit the gym after work. 퇴근 후에 헬스하러 가자.

Power walking burns more calories than running. 파워 워킹이 러닝보다 칼로리를 더 많이 연소한다.

You should stretch before and after a workout. 운동 전후에 스트레칭을 해야 한다.

She has a very fast metabolism. 그녀는 신진대사가 매우 빠르다.

3 times per week is said to be ideal for strength training. 근력 운동은 주당 3회가 이상적이라고 한다.

It was a waste of time.
시간 낭비였어.

 천사표

~stinks: ~는 형편없다, 후지다

That movie stinks.
그 영화 엄청 구려.

Kell2013

The 3D conversion?
3D로 나온 거?

 천사표

ridiculous 터무니없는, 우스꽝스러운

I'm not a big fan of 3D movies, but this is ridiculous.
3D 영화를 좋아하는 편은 아니지만, 이건 말도 안돼.

Kell2013

Did you see the original version?
오리지널 판 봤어?

 천사표

Sure. Who didn't?
그럼. 안 본 사람도 있나?

Kell2013

How many times did you see it?
그 영화 몇 번 봤어?

 천사표
Twice in the cinema, several more times on DVD and cable.
글쎄, 극장에서 두 번, DVD랑 케이블에서 몇 번.

🔑 kill excitement: 흥미를 잃게 하다   Kell2013
That must have killed the excitement of the remake?!
그니까 리메이크가 재미없었겠지!

 천사표   🔑 It was a waste of time.: 시간 낭비였어.
It was a waste of time, anyway.
하여간 시간 낭비였어.

Kell2013
Sorry to hear that.
그렇다니 유감이네.

 천사표   🔑 take a nap: 낮잠자다
I should have taken a nice long nap instead.
그럴 시간에 낮잠이나 실컷 잘걸.

 영화와 관련된 표현

What's on at the cinema? 그 영화관에서 무슨 영화 상영하니?
What's the movie about? 그 영화 내용은 뭐야?
Who's it starring? 누가 주연인데?
Wanna get some popcorn? Salted or sweet? 팝콘 먹을까? 짭짤한 맛 아님 달콤한 맛?
Anything to drink? 마실 건?

ChitChat 082

No wonder you're so good at English!
그래서 그렇게 영어를 잘 하는구나!

백조
I hate practicing for English interviews!
영어 인터뷰 연습하기 넘 싫어!

🖉 Wanna come to~ = Do you want to come to~ / convo = conversation

빈
Wanna come to my English convo group?
우리 영어회화 그룹에 들어올래?

백조
English convo group?
영어회화 그룹이라구?

빈
We meet up twice a month and practice English over dinner and drinks.
한 달에 두 번 만나서 저녁 식사와 술을 마시면서 영어 연습을 해.

백조
No wonder you're so good at English!
그래서 그렇게 영어를 잘하는구나!

🖉 give it a shot: 한번 해보다 / simultaneously: 동시에

빈
You should give it a shot. You can make new friends, eat good food n study English simultaneously.
너도 한번 해봐. 새 친구도 사귀고, 맛난 음식에 영어공부까지 동시에 할 수 있어.

🖉 be better off ~: ~하는 게 낫다 / take classes: 수업 듣다, 수강하다

백조
Maybe I'm better off taking classes. There's a place near my house...
난 걍 수업 듣는 게 나을 듯해. 우리 집 근처에 학원이 하나 있거든...

빈

🎵 ur: you're

We're currently accepting new members.
If ur interested let me know.
현재 신입 회원 모집 중인데. 관심 있음 알려줘.

백조

🎵 shy: 숫기가 없는, 붙임성이 없는, 부끄러워 하는

I'm a little shy around new faces… It might be really awkward.
난 모르는 사람들 앞에서 좀 부끄러움을 타는데…정말 어색할지도 몰라.

🎵 get over: 극복하다

빈

I hear ya. I was at first too but everyone is so nice you get over it real quick!
알긋따. 나도 첨엔 그랬는데 다들 넘 나이스해서 진짜 금방 괜찮아질 거야.

백조

Ok then. I'll give it a try!
글탐 좋아. 해볼 테야!

빈

Yay!!!
예이!!!

More to Talk!

새로운 사람들과의 만남에 관한 표현

I feel awkward in a room full of people I don't know. 모르는 사람들이 우글거리는 방에 있음 뻘쭘해.

How can I start a conversation at a party where I don't know anyone? 아무도 아는 사람이 없는 파티에서 어떻게 대화를 시작할 수 있을까?

She can easily walk up to a stranger and start chatting. 그녀는 모르는 사람에게 쉽게 다가가 수다를 떨 수 있다.

We've only met a few times but he feels like an old friend. 몇 번밖에 안 만났지만 그는 오랜 친구처럼 느껴진다.

Meeting people in person that you've met online can be dangerous! 온라인에서 만난 사람들을 직접 만나는 것은 위험할 수도 있어!

That's my show!
내가 정말 좋아하는 프로그램이야!

🎤 **episode**: 1회 방송분

천사표
Did you see last night's episode of Queen of Beauty?
어젯밤 '미의 여왕' 봤니?

🎤 **show**: (방송) 프로, 프로그램

백조
U watch it too?! OMG That's my show!
너도 봤니?! 어머. 그거 내가 정말 좋아하는 프로야.

천사표
I don't think I can wait until next week's episode...
다음 주 방송까지 못 기다릴 것 같아…

🎤 **cliffhanger**: 서스펜스가 지속되는 드라마, 손에 땀을 쥐게 되는 상황

백조
Me neither. I hate cliffhangers like that.
나두. 난 그렇게 조마조마한 건 딱 질색이야.

천사표
Yeah seriously. And when are they going to kiss already?!!?!?!
응 완전. 그리고 키스는 도대체 언제 하는 거야?

🎤 **drag out**: 질질 끌다

백조
I know, right!? How long are they going to drag this out?
그치, 응? 얼마나 질질 끌 셈일까?

 천사표

🎤 get a contract w/: get a contract with, ~와 계약하다

BTW, did you hear the actor that plays Haneul got a contract w/ 'M' Makeup?
그건 그렇고, '하늘'역 맡은 배우가 '엠' 화장품 회사와 계약한 거 들었어?

🎤 It's no surprise.: 당연하다, 놀랄 것이 없다. / stunning: 기절할 만큼 아름다운   백조

It's no surprise. She is stunning after all.
놀랄 것도 없지. 기절하게 예쁘니까.

 천사표

I heard she's also appearing on a variety show Tuesday night.
화요일 밤에 버라이어티 쇼에도 나올 거라고 하더라.

🎤 be a huge fan of ~: ~의 광 팬이다, ~를 너무 좋아한다   백조

I'll have to tune in. I'm a huge fan of hers.
채널 고정해야겠네. 나 짱팬이거든.

 TV와 관련된 표현

Daytime soap operas are absolutely addictive! 낮에 하는 드라마들은 완전 중독성이 있어!

You ordered another item off the home shopping channel? 너 홈쇼핑 채널에서 또 상품 주문했구나.

I am going to hurry home to try to catch tonight's game. 오늘밤 게임을 보기 위해 집으로 서둘러 가야 해.

There are so many commercials for skin creams. 피부용 크림 광고가 너무 많다.

Can you see what else is on? This is boring. 딴 거 뭐 하는지 봐줄래? 이거 지루해.

 084

Just the thought of it makes me cringe. 생각만 해도 민망해.

Tae
My boss is irritated with me.
보스가 나한테 짜증내고 있어.

King_Michael
What did you do now? Lol
뭘 했길래? ㅋㅋㅋ

 Tae
🔖 ur = you're
I went home before my coworkers went to a singing room last night.
어젯밤에 노래방에 동료들이 다 모이기도 전에 내가 집에 와버렸거든.

🔖 shoulda just gone: should have just gone **King_Michael**
You shoulda just gone.
그냥 가지 그랬어.

 Tae
🔖 cringe: 움찔해지는, 민망한
And sing in front of everyone? Just the thought of it makes me cringe.
그래서 모든 사람들 앞에서 노래하라고? 생각만 해도 민망해.

🔖 make an excuse: 변명하다 **King_Michael**
It looks bad to be the first person to leave. Did u make a good excuse at least?
젤 먼저 일어나면 안 좋게 보이지. 적어도 그럴 듯하게 변명은 했지?

Tae

I pretended to be drunk but everyone knows I really wasn't.
취한 척하긴 했지만 다들 아닌 거 알아.

🎵 get over one's fear: 공포를 극복하다 / b/4: before   **King_Michael**

You're going to have to get over your fear b/4 everyone at work hates u.
직장 동료들이 몽땅 너를 미워하기 전에 니 공포증부터 극복을 해야겠다.

 Tae

🎵 sign up for ~: ~를 등록하다

That's why I signed up for singing lessons this morning.
그래서 오늘 아침에 보컬 레슨 등록했어.

King_Michael

Good thinking.
잘 생각했다.

 **More to Talk!**

 노래방 관련 표현

You can order more beer if you like. 원한다면 맥주를 더 시켜도 돼.

My boss usually wears his tie on his head when he has a few too many.
우리 보스는 좀 과하게 마시면 보통 머리에 넥타이를 맨다.

If you can't sing, dance and play the tambourine instead! 노래 못하면 그 대신 춤추고 탬버린이라도 쳐!.

There are lots of English songs to choose from. 영어로 된 노래 고를 거 많아.

Once you pick your song, enter the number like this. 노래를 고르고 나면 이런 식으로 번호를 입력해.

I hate when somebody ruins the fun atmosphere with some sappy ballad. 난 누군가가 처지는 발라드로 신나는 분위기 깰 때 너무 싫더라.

ChitChat 085

I feel like an entirely new person.
다시 태어난 기분이야.

백조
Hey, can you tell me the name of your yoga studio again?
안녕, 니가 다니는 요가 스튜디오 이름이 뭐랬지?

빈
Lotus Yoga
로터스 요가

백조
Ah, right. Thanks!
응. 고마워!

🔖 facilities: 시설물

빈
You're going to love it! Their teachers are so professional and the facilities are all brand new.
맘에 들 거야! 거기 선생님들은 정말 전문적이고 시설은 완전 새삥이야.

백조
Really?
정말?

빈
Yeah, they just renovated the whole building. It's fantastic.
응, 빌딩 전체를 막 리모델링했거든. 완전 짱이야.

백조
Cool.
쪼은데.

빈
The prices aren't bad either. If you sign up for three months you get a 30% discount. I did a whole year and got a free mat and some other yoga gear.
수강료도 나쁘지 않아. 3개월 끊으면 30퍼센트 할인해줘. 1년치 끊으니 매트랑 다른 요가 용품을 주더라.

백조
Neat.
좋은데.

♪ 2 kilos: 2 kilograms

Since starting I've lost 2 kilos, my skin has gotten clearer, and my back doesn't hurt anymore!
시작하고 나서 2킬로 빠지고 피부는 한결 더 깨끗해지고 허리도 더 이상 아프지 않아!

That's great news.
정말 잘됐다.

♪ A.M.: 오전

I feel like an entirely new person! So which class are you going to take? A.M. Beginners?
다시 태어난 기분이야! 그럼 어떤 수업을 받으려고? 오전 초보반?

Oh I just needed the name for my GPS. I want to go to the bookstore next door but can't remember the name.
아, 난 그냥 GPS땜에 이름이 필요했어. 그 옆에 있는 서점에 가고 싶은데 이름이 기억이 안 나가지고.

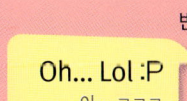

Oh... Lol :P
아… ㅋㅋㅋ

More to Talk!

단체 가입, 등록 관련 표현

They offer a one month free trial for new members. 신입 회원에게 1개월 자유 이용권을 제공해.

I registered for flower arranging classes at the florist down the street.
길 아래 꽃집에서 꽃꽂이 수업에 등록했다.

Their hiking club goes to a different mountain every other Saturday.
그들의 하이킹 클럽은 격주 토요일마다 다른 산으로 간다.

If you can't meet up in person then try joining an online community.
직접 만날 수 없다면 온라인 커뮤니티에 가입해봐.

A book club seems like a great way to think more deeply about important issues. 북 클럽은 중요한 사안에 대해 한층 깊이 생각할 수 있는 아주 좋은 방법인 거 같아.

Where is your sense of adventure? 모험심은 어쨌어?

 Tae

Any interest in going to Jeju this summer vacation?
이번 여름방학 때 제주도나 갈까 하는 데 관심 있어?

🔖 **way behind:** 너무 뒤처진, 너무 밀린

King_Michael

I don't know... I'm way behind on my studies.
몰겠어… 공부할 게 넘 밀려서.

 Tae

🔖 **Ur: You're / pass up:** 포기하다, 거절하다

Seriously?
Ur gonna pass up this trip to go to some academy again?
진심? 또 무슨 학원 땜에 이 여행을 포기한다고?

 Tae

Think about the girls!
여자애들을 상상해봐!

King_Michael

What girls? You guys are gonna be surfing the whole time...
뭔 여자애들? 너네 종일 서핑만 할 거잖아.

 Tae

🔖 **BBQ;** 바베큐(파티 하다), 고기 구워 먹다

Not the WHOLE time.
We'll be BBQing and drinking after sunset ;)
"종일"은 아니지. 해지면 고기 구워 먹고 술 마실 거야.

🔖 tempting. 유혹적인. 끌리는　　King_Michael

Hmm...it's tempting but...
음... 땡기긴 하는데...

Tae

But what?
근데 뭐?

🔖 beef up: 보강하다, 강화하다　　King_Michael

I've got to beef up my resume before I graduate.
졸업 전에 이력서도 보강해야 해.

Tae

🔖 sense of adventure: 모험심 / refresh: 재충전하다

Bro, where is your sense of adventure? Sand, sun, sea... girls. You need to refresh before next semester.
친구, 모험심 어디 갔냐? 모래, 태양, 바다… 여자애들. 담 학기 되기 전에 재충전해야지.

🔖 count ~ in: ~를 끼워주다　　King_Michael

Yeah... alright. Count me in.
그래… 좋아. 나도 껴줘.

 호의를 사양하는 표현

Well, the thing is… I've already made other plans. 실은 말야… 이미 다른 계획들을 세워놨거든.

I want to, but I'm afraid I can't. 그러고 싶지만 안돼.

It seems like a good idea, but I don't think it'll work. 좋은 생각 같긴 한데, 안될 거 같아.

I want to… but I really can't. 그러고 싶긴 한데, 정말 안되겠어.

I see what you're saying but I'll have to disagree. 니가 무슨 말 하는지 알겠지만 난 반대해야겠어.

Review — Words & Expressions — CHAT 07

ChitChat 076 — p 188
Bored out of my mind.

(I'm) Bored out of my mind. 지루해서 미치겠어.
sit in 방콕하다, 집에만 있다
Wanna? 그럴래?
ride a bike 자전거 타다
kite 연
fly a kite 연 날리다
gather 모이다
sand castle 모래성
tan 태닝
ballpark 야구장
Cherry Blossom Festival 벚꽃 축제
go on a double date 쌍쌍 데이트 가다

ChitChat 077 — p 190
I haven't gone anywhere in ages.

I can't afford it. 그럴 여유 없어
sis(sister) 여자 형제
homemaking 집안 일
work 24/7 밤낮을 가리지 않고 일하다
It's bad timing. 시기가 좋지 않아.
Maybe some other time. 다음에 기회 봐서.
You tell me. 내 말이, 그러니까
I haven't gone anywhere in ages. 어디론가 떠나본 지가 언젠지 몰라.
We'll see. 봐서.
See you in 20. 20분 있다가 보자.
Can I take a rain check? 이 다음에 할 수 있을까?
Don't be a stranger. 연락하고 지내자.

ChitChat 078 — p 192
He's an athletic freak.

talk nonsense 말도 안 되는 이야기를 하다
give advice 조언 해주다
well-informed 박식한
athletic freak 운동광
He's an athletic freak. 그는 운동광이야.
well-built 몸이 다부진
Don't rub it in. 불 난 데 부채질 하지 마.
It's on me. 내가 쏠게.
treadmill 러닝 머신
run on the treadmill 러닝 머신에서 뛰다
footwear 신발
joint 관절
protect your joints 관절을 보호하다
workout routine 운동 절차
set up the workout routine 운동 절차를 정하다
Stay hydrated. 계속 물을 마셔.
6-pack abs 빨래판 복근

ChitChat 079 — p 194
I'm drawn to baking classes.

certified barista 공인된 바리스타
I have mixed feelings. 복잡한 기분이야.
coffee place 커피 집
expertise 전문 지식
picture oneself 상상하다
I can't picture ~ ~하는 것이 상상이 안 된다
run a bakery 베이커리를 운영하다
I'm drawn to baking classes. 베이킹 수업에 관심이 가네.

at least 적어도
temp 임시직
9-to-5ers 정규 직원
quality time 양질의 시간

ChitChat 080 — p 196
Let's get together more often.

That was a blast. 너무 재미있었어.
fat burning 지방 연소
stress relief 스트레스 해소
killing two birds with one stone 일석이조
muscular 근육의
I know. 맞아, 그러니까.
positive outlet 긍정적인 배출구
fit and healthy 튼튼하고 건강한
Hear! Hear! 옳소! 옳소!
Hit the gym. 헬쓰 하러 가다
after work 퇴근 후
calories 칼로리
metabolism 신진 대사
strength training 근력 운동

ChitChat 081 — p 198
It was a waste of time.

a big fan of ~ ~의 열렬한 팬
cinema 영화관
kill the excitement 흥미를 잃게 하다
waste of time 시간 낭비
nap 낮잠
take a nap 낮잠 자다
Who's it starring? 누가 주인공인데?

ChitChat 082 — p 200
No wonder you're so good at English!

convo conversation의 약자, 대화
No wonder you're so good at English. 그래서 영어를 그렇게 잘하는구나.
give it a shot 시험삼아 한번 해보다
simultaneously 동시에
be better off ~하는 게 더 낫다
currently 현재
shy 붙임성 없는, 부끄러워하는
get over 극복하다

ChitChat 083 — p 202
That's my show!

show (방송) 프로그램
That's my show. 내가 좋아하는 프로그램이야.
cliffhanger 손에 땀을 쥐게 되는 상황
drag out 질질 끌다
get a contract with ~ ~와 계약하다
It's no surprise. 놀랄 것도 없다.
stunning 엄청난
variety show 버라이어티 쇼
soap opera 드라마
addictive 중독성이 있는
commercial (방송) 광고
What else is on? 딴 건(방송은) 뭐하니?

CHAT 07

ChitChat 084 — p 204
Just the thought of it makes me cringe.

irritated with ~ ~때문에 짜증난
coworker 회사 동료
singing room 노래방
Just thought of it makes me cringe. 생각만 해도 민망해.
cringe 민망한, 움찔해지는
excuse 변명
make an excuse 변명하다
pretend to be drunk 술 취한 척 하다
fear 공포
singing lessons 본컬 레슨
tambourine 탬버린
ruin the fun atmosphere 분위기를 망치다
sappy 감성적인
ballad 발라드

ChitChat 085 — p 206
I feel like an entirely new person.

yoga 요가
professional 프로다운
facilities 시설물
brand new 완전 새로운
renovate: 보수하다
get a discount 할인 받다
yoga gear 요가 용품
Neat! 멋지다! 좋아!
lose 2 kilos 2킬로그램 빠지다

I feel like an entirely new person. 다시 태어난 기분이야. 완전 새 사람 된 기분이야.
book store 서점
free trial 무료 체험
register for ~ ~에 등록하다
flower arranging classes 꽃꽂이 반
florist 꽃집
every other Saturday 격주로 토요일 마다
In person 직접

ChitChat 086 — p 208
Where is your sense of adventure?

behind on one's studies ~의 공부가 뒤처지다, 밀리다
pass up 포기하다, 거절하다
academy 학원
BBQ 바비큐(파티하다), 고기를 구워먹다
after sunset 해가 진 후에
tempting 유혹적인, 끌리는
beef up 보강하다, 강화하다
Where is your sense of adventure? 모험심은 어쨌어?
refresh 재충전하다
semester 학기
Count me in. 나도 껴줘.
make plans 계획을 세우다
disagree 반대하다

CHAT 08

Everyday Life and Problems

일상 생활 및 문제점

- 087 What am I? Chopped liver?
- 088 Cutting food waste helps Korea go greener.
- 089 She never throws anything away.
- 090 I got caught jaywalking.
- 091 Just for kicks.
- 092 I'm already regretting it.
- 093 It's like the 7th solid day of rain.
- 094 Maybe he has some other issue.
- 095 Guys, bundle up.
- 096 Not in a million years.
- 097 I had my fortune told.
- 098 It cost me an arm and a leg.
- 099 She's a super haggler.
- 100 I'll have to eat and run.

What am I? Chopped liver? 난 뭐데? 별볼 일 없어?

동분서주

🎵 bf: boy friend의 약자, 남친

My new bf is smart, funny, and handsome... but...
내 새 남친은 스마트하고 재미나고 핸섬하긴 한데…

Jas

So?
그래서?

동분서주

🎵 inconsistent: 일관성이 없는 / absent-minded: 딴 데 정신 팔려 있는, 건망증이 심한

He's so inconsistent and absent-minded!
넘 일관성이 없고 딴 데 정신 팔려 있어!

Jas

I guess you can't have it all.
다 갖출 수야 있나.

동분서주

He totally forgot my birthday today!
내 생일을 완전 까먹은 거 있지!

🎵 BTW: by the way / b-day: birthday의 약자, 생일 Jas

Oh, BTW, happy b-day!
아, 그건 그렇고 생일 축하해!

동분서주 　I don't care about you.: 넌 상관없어.

Oh I don't care about you!
어, 그러거나 말거나!

chopped liver: 별 볼일 없는 사람(것), 무의미한 사람(것) 　Jas

What am I? Chopped liver?
난 뭔데? 별 볼일 없어?

동분서주

You know what I mean!
내 말 알잖아!

 Like I said.: 말했듯이, 얘기했지. 　Jas

So kind. Like I said, you can't have it all.
참 착하기도 하네. 말했지, 전부 다 가질 순 없다고.

More to Talk!

 요구와 관련된 표현

Is that too much to ask? 그게 무리한 요구야?
That sounds too much to ask of him. 그에게 그런 요구를 하는 건 무리야.
Just name it. I'll get it for you. 말만 해. 다 갖다 바칠게.
Do it! Would it kill you or what? 해! 그럼 죽기라도 해?
Don't bite off more than you can chew. 한꺼번에 너무 욕심 내지 마.

Cutting food waste helps Korea go greener. 음식물 쓰레기 줄이면 한국의 환경 오염을 줄일 수 있어.

 천사표
R u using food trash bags too?
너도 음식물 쓰레기 봉투 사용하고 있니?

Jas
What?
뭐?

천사표
Food trash bags.
음식물 쓰레기 봉투.

 ♪nah: no의 구어 표현 Jas
Nah. I separate the other trash though.
아니. 그래도 다른 쓰레기는 분리해.

 천사표
♪disposable (plastic) bags: 일회용 (비닐) 봉투 / convenience store: 편의점
**You're supposed to bag your food waste.
They sell disposable bags at convenience stores.**
음식물 쓰레기를 봉투에 담아야 해. 편의점 같은 데서 일회용 봉투를 팔거든.

♪I C: I see의 인터넷 약어 Jas
I C. It's a practical way to help reduce the amount of food garbage.
글쿤. 음식물 쓰레기 양을 줄이는 데 실제적으로 도움이 될 수 있겠네.

 천사표 🔖 Indeed: 정말 그래. 그렇다마다

Indeed.
그렇다마다.

🔖 pay attention to ~: ~에 관심을 갖다   Jas

I should pay more attention to that.
좀 더 관심을 기울여야 하겠네.

 천사표

They say cutting food waste helps Korea go greener.
음식물 쓰레기를 줄이면 한국의 환경오염을 줄일 수 있다잖아.

Jas

Yeah, you should do your part as a citizen.
그래. 시민으로서 지킬 건 지켜야지.

More to Talk!

 환경보호에 관한 표현

Be sure to dry out your food waste before taking it out. 음식물 쓰레기는 버리기 전에 반드시 말리도록 해.

Check your fridge and plan your meals before grocery shopping. 장보기 전에 냉장고를 확인하고 메뉴를 짜봐.

Don't scrape leftovers into the bin. Instead, use them as ingredients for the next meal. 남은 음식을 긁어서 쓰레기 통에 버리지 마. 대신 그걸 다음 끼니 재료로 활용해봐.

Make it a habit to freeze any leftover food. 남은 음식은 냉동하는 습관을 들여.

Try to cook only as much as you can eat. 먹을 수 있을 만큼만 요리해.

 ChitChat 089

She never throws anything away.
그녀는 도무지 버리질 않아.

 동분서주
U know June?
준 알지?

🎵 roomie: 룸메이트 Kell2013
Ur roomie?
니 룸메이트?

 동분서주   🎵 odd: 특이한, 남다른
Yes. She's odd.
응. 걔 좀 특이해.

 Kell2013
How odd?
어떻게 특이한데?

 동분서주   🎵 throw away: 버리다
She never throws anything away.
절대 아무것도 안 버려.

 Kell2013
Really?
정말?

 동분서주   🎵 inaccessible: 접근하기 어려운
Her room is overflowing with stuff n completely inaccessible.
방에 물건이 가득 차서 들어갈 수도 없어.

♪ hoarder: 병적으로 축적하는 사람, 축적가, 호더

Kell2013

What a hoarder!
완전 호더구나!

 동분서주

♪ every single day: 매일매일

Plus more boxes come in every single day.
게다가 맨날 박스가 오는 거야.

Kell2013

Sounds serious.
심각한 거 같네.

 동분서주

♪ break down the wall: 벽을 부수다

Someday I'll need to break down the wall to reach her.
언젠가 걜 보려면 벽을 부숴야 할 거 같아.

♪ gimme a break = give me a break: 그럴 리가, 설마

Kell2013

Haha. Gimme a break. It can't be that bad!
하하. 설마. 그렇게 심하겠니!

More to Talk!

 집 정리, 청소 등에 관련된 표현

His house is cluttered with comic books. 그의 집은 만화책으로 어지럽혀져 있다.

I've never seen such a neat and tidy person as him. 난 그 남자처럼 깔끔하고 정리 잘하는 사람 본 적 없어.

Her place is squeaky clean. 그녀의 집은 먼지 하나 없이 깨끗해.

I can't put up with a messy person like you. 너처럼 너저분한 사람은 더 이상 못 참겠다.

It's been 2 months since I moved, but I haven't started unpacking yet.
이사한 지 2달이나 됐는데 아직 짐 푸는 건 시작도 못했어.

ChitChat 090

I got caught jaywalking.
무단 횡단하다 걸렸어.

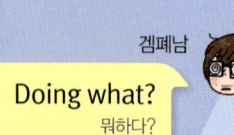

 Jas
> I got busted.
> 딱 걸렸어.

겜폐남
> Doing what?
> 뭐하다?

 Jas
🎵 jaywalking: 무단 횡단
> I got caught jaywalking.
> 무단횡단하다 걸렸어.

🎵 straight shooter: 법 없이도 살 사람, 솔직하고 정직한 사람   겜폐남
> And here I thought you were a straight shooter.
> 넌 법 없이도 살 줄 알았는데.

 Jas
🎵 have no choice: 여지가 없다, 어쩔 수 없다 / be in a rush: 바쁘다
> I had no choice. I was in a rush.
> 어쩔 수 없었어. 급한 일이 있었거든.

🎵 pay a fine: 벌금 내다   겜폐남
> I guess you'll have to pay a fine?
> 벌금 내야겠네?

Jas

🎵 cut ~ some slack: ~를 좀 봐주다

The police officer cut me some slack.
경찰이 좀 봐줬어.

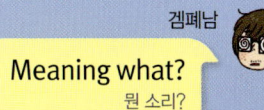 겜폐남

Meaning what?
뭔 소리?

 Jas

🎵 warning: 경고, 훈방

He let me go with a warning this time. :)
이번엔 경고만 하고 보내줬다고.

 겜폐남

Well aren't you lucky!!!
운 좋았네!!!

 More to Talk!

 교통 위반과 관련된 표현

He ran the red light. 그 남자는 빨간 불을 무시하고 달렸다.

The police gave him a speeding ticket. 경찰이 그에게 속도위반 딱지를 끊었다.

She slammed on the brakes not to hit the pedestrian. 그녀는 보행자를 치지 않으려고 급정거했다.

He's a victim of a hit and run. 그는 뺑소니 사고의 피해자다.

I had to pay a fine for illegal parking. 불법 주차로 벌금을 냈어.

ChitChat 091

Just for kicks.
걍 재미로.

Kell2013
🔊 reunion: 동창회
Did I tell you I was at the high school reunion yesterday?
어제 고등학교 동창회 갔었다고 얘기했나?

천사표
Wow. It's not like U.
와~. 너답지 않은데.

Kell2013
🔊 for kicks: 재미로
I know. Just for kicks.
그니까. 걍 재미로.

🔊 What did I miss?: 내가 놓친 것 있어? 새로운 거 있어?
천사표
So, what did I miss?
새로운 거 있었어?

Kell2013
🔊 squeaky: 빽빽거리는, (듣기 싫은) 끼익 소리를 내는
Remember Eugene with the high squeaky voice?
하이톤으로 빽빽거리던 유진 기억나?

천사표
Sure do.
당근.

Kell2013
🔊 remarry: 재혼하다
He remarried his ex-wife.
전처랑 재결합했대.

천사표
Wow. That is new.
와. 참신한 소식인데.

 Kell2013
And Young's expecting his third baby.
영은 셋째가 곧 태어날 거래.

천사표
Attaboy!!!
장하네!!!

 Kell2013
Haha.
하하.

🖊 juicy: 재미있는, 즙이 많은   천사표
Any other juicy stories?
다른 거 재밌는 건?

 Kell2013   🖊 sweetheart: 애인
Like the one about ur high school sweetheart?
네가 고딩 때 사귀던 애인 얘기 같은 거?

🖊 Who cares!: 관심 없어, 알 게 뭐야.   천사표
Whoa! He chose Yoori over me. Who cares?
그만! 나 말고 유리를 택했는데. 알 게 뭐야?

More to Talk!

 결혼과 관련된 표현

My ex invited me to his engagement party. 내 구남친이 자기 약혼식에 나를 초대했다.
They are known for splitting up. 그들은 별거한 것으로 알려져 있다.
Where's the wedding reception? 피로연은 어디니?
He decided to remarry for his son. 그는 아들을 위해 재혼을 결심했다.
Marriages of convenience are nothing new. 정략결혼은 어제오늘 일이 아니다.

ChitChat 092

I'm already regretting it.
벌써 후회가 돼.

 천사표
> Ask me who I saw today.
> 나 오늘 누구 봤는지 물어봐.

Kell2013
> Who?
> 누군데?

 천사표
> Chan from Boy's Generation!!
> 소년시대의 찬!!

 Kell2013
> Oh, was he cute?
> 멋있던?

 천사표

🎵 star-struck: (연예인에게) 완전히 푹 빠진

> I got star-struck! I almost walked into a pole.
> 완전 뿅~ 갔어! 거의 전봇대에 부딪칠 뻔했다니까.

Kell2013
> lol
> ㅋㅋ

 천사표
> He he
> 헤헤

🎵 autograph: 사인

Kell2013
Get an autograph?
사인 받았어?

천사표 🎵 Nope: No의 구어체 표현

Nope!
아닛!

Kell2013
Why not?
왜?

천사표 🎵 tacky: 촌스러운, 저속한 / celeb: celebrity의 줄임말

It's tacky to ask a celeb for an autograph.
연예인한테 사인해달라는 거 촌스러워.

🎵 once-in-a-lifetime chance: 일생에 한번 찾아올까 말까 한 기회   Kell2013

Could have been your once-in-a-lifetime chance to meet him, though.
그래도 평생 다시 안올 기회였을지도 모르잖아.

천사표 🎵 regret: 후회하다

Actually, I'm already regretting it.
사실 벌써 후회하고 있어.

💡 확률, 기회를 활용한 표현

More to Talk!

Not a chance. 어림 없어.
Why not take a chance? 운에 맡겨봐.
You have no chance of getting her back. 그녀를 되찾을 승산은 없어.
I'll take a chance on that. 한번 모험해볼까 봐.
Luckily enough, I got a second chance. 운 좋게도 난 기회를 한 번 더 얻게 됐어.

ChitChat 093

It's like the 7th solid day of rain.
7일 내리 비가 오는 셈이네.

백조: I'm bored!!!
심심해!!!

🎵 ~ or something: ~같은 거
빈: Do some shopping or something.
쇼핑이라도 해.

백조: I am already. Hehe.
이미 쇼핑 중야. 헤헤.

빈: Where at?
어디야?

백조: We-Dome.
웨돔.

빈: Wish I were there with you.
나도 거기 같이 있음 얼마나 좋을까.

🎵 likewise: 마찬가지야, 나도 그래
백조: Likewise.
나두.

🎵 drizzling: 보슬비가 내리는, 이슬비가 오는
빈: Uhh, looks like it's drizzling out.
밖에 보슬비가 오는 거 같아.

 백조
Not here... Oh, no!!!
여긴 아닌데… 아, 안돼!!!

 빈
What's wrong?
왜 그래?

 백조
🔍 **pouring**: 퍼붓는, 쏟아져 내리는
It started pouring.
퍼붓기 시작했어.

 빈
🔍 **clear up**: (비 등이) 개다
Wait inside there until it clears up.
갤 때까지 거기 안에서 기다려.

 백조
Yeah. It's like the 7th sold day of rain. :'(
응. 7일 내리 비가 오는 셈이네 ㅠㅠ

 빈
🔍 **sick of ~**: ~이 싫증난, 지겨운
I know! I'm sick of it!!!
그러게! 지겨워!!!

More to Talk!

 비와 관련된 표현

It's raining cats and dogs. 비가 억수같이 퍼붓고 있어.

I stepped in a puddle and now my shoes are all wet. 웅덩이를 밟아서 신발이 쫄딱 젖었어.

The rainy season seems especially long this year. 올해 장마는 유난히 긴 것 같아.

I feel like eating bindaetteok and Makkoli whenever it rains. 비 올 때마다 빈대떡과 막걸리가 먹고 싶어.

I was caught in heavy rain. 폭우 때문에 꼼짝 못했어.

I don't mind walking in light rain. 보슬비가 올 땐 걷는 것도 상관없어.

ChitChat

Maybe he has some other issue. 뭔가 다른 문제가 있겠지.

 천사표
> Vic is such a pain.
> 빅 때문에 진짜 짜증나.

Kell2013
> What did he do this time?
> 요번엔 뭘 했는데?

 천사표
> He just pooped on my rug.
> 방금 러그에 똥 쌌어.

Kell2013
> Oh, no. That was really pricey too...
> 안 돼. 게다가 그거 진짜 비싼 거였잖아...

 천사표
> I've done everything I can.
> 난 할 수 있는 만큼 다 했어.

🖊 potty training: 배변 훈련

Kell2013
> He has no problem other than the potty training.
> 배변 훈련 말고는 아무 문제 없잖아.

 천사표
> True. But that's driving me crazy.
> 맞아. 근데 그것 때문에 미치겠어.

Kell2013

Maybe he has some other issue.
뭔가 다른 문제가 있겠지.

천사표

Know any reliable obedience school?
믿을 만한 애견 훈련소 아는 데 있어?

Kell2013

Let me ask around.
알아볼게.

천사표

I should do something before it's too late.
너무 늦기 전에 뭔가 해야겠어.

Kell2013

 **Good thinking.**
좋은 생각이다.

 애완동물과 관련된 표현

I usually walk my puppy every day for about half an hour. 난 보통 매일 30분씩 강아지를 산책시켜.

R U a cat person or a dog person? 고양이를 좋아해 아님 개를 좋아해?

He recently adopted an abandoned dog. 그는 최근에 유기견을 입양했어.

Pets come with big responsibilities. 애완동물은 큰 책임감이 따르지.

He uses his cute puppy to pick up girls. 그는 여자 꼬시는 데 자신의 귀여운 강아지를 이용해.

Guys, bundle up.
얘들아, 껴입어.

동분서주

freezing cold: 얼어붙을 듯 추운

I heard it's freezing cold outside.
오늘 밖에 무지 춥다는데.

천사표

Yeah. I heard that, too.
응. 나도 들었어.

Kell2013

Let's go see a movie and then do some shopping.
영화 보고 쇼핑이나 하자.

동분서주

Did you guys reserve tickets?
영화표 예약은 했어?

matinee: 주간에 하는 공연·상영   천사표

Yeah, we booked a 4:30 matinee.
응, 오후 4시 30분 거 예매했어.

Kell2013

grab a dinner: 저녁 먹다

Then let's grab dinner after.
보고 나서 저녁 먹자.

동분서주

Great. Let's hang inside.
좋아. 실내에서 놀자.

bundle up: 껴입다

 천사표

Bundle up, guys!
껴입어, 얘들아!

 동분서주

I'm not worried. We're gonna go to an indoor mall!
걱정할 거 없어. 실내에 있는 쇼핑몰에 갈 건데!

 Kell2013

nice and cozy: 완전 아늑한

And the movie theater should be nice and cozy as well!
글구 영화관은 완전 아늑할 건데 뭐.

 동분서주

천사표

Yayyyyy. Finally we're all hanging out!!!
예이~~~~. 드뎌 우리 모두 만나네!!!

More to Talk!

 실내 활동에 관한 표현

Let's stay in until it clears up. 날이 갤 때까지 안에 있자.

We're so different. He's a homebody and I like to go out. 우린 넘 달라. 그는 집에 있는 걸 좋아하고 난 밖에서 시간 보내는 걸 좋아해.

I stayed cooped up inside all weekend but at least I finished my novel.
주말 내내 방에 콕 박혀 있었지만 적어도 그 소설책은 다 읽었어.

I really want to minimize time spent doing housework. 나 정말 집안일 하면서 보내는 시간을 최소화하고 싶어.

He started wearing that stupid belly fat burner belt all around the house.
그는 집안 어디서든 그 우스꽝스러워 보이는 복부 지방을 태우는 벨트를 착용하기 시작했어.

 **096**

Not in a million years.
절대 안 해.

Kell2013
> What happened?
> 무슨 일이야?

> I got into a little car accident.
> 접촉사고 났어.

천사표

Kell2013

📎 OMG: Oh, my god의 인터넷 용어

> OMG. Did you get hurt?
> 다쳤어?

> No.
> 아니.

천사표

Kell2013
> Thank goodness.
> 다행이다.

📎 claim to be injured: 상해를 당했다고 주장하다, 다쳤다고 주장하다

> But the other driver claimed to be injured.
> 근데 상대측 운전자가 다쳤다고 우기는 거야.

천사표

📎 fender bender: 접촉사고 / No biggie: No big deal 별일 아니야, 큰일이야 있겠니

> It was just a fender bender. No biggie.
> 강 접촉사고였으니까. 별일은 없겠지만.

천사표

Kell2013
How did it happen?
어쩌다 그랬어?

천사표
I had to swerve to avoid hitting a stray dog.
길 잃은 개를 치지 않으려고 방향을 바꿔야 했어.

 Kell2013
Is it okay?
개는 괜찮아?

천사표
Yes.
응.

 Kell2013
🔍 **a stroke of luck**: 운수 대통, 요행, 천우신조
It was a stroke of luck for him.
진짜 운 좋았다.

🔍 **Not in a million years**: 절대 안해, 다신 안할 거야
I'll never drive again!! Not in a million years!!!
운전 안 해!! 절대 다신 안 할 거야!!!

 **More to Talk!**

 교통사고와 관련된 표현

He junked his car after the car crash. 그는 자동차 사고 이후에 차를 폐차시켰어.

She was a victim of the head-on collision. 그녀는 정면 충돌 사고 피해자야.

Your car insurance will cover the theft. 네 자동차 보험이 절도를 보상할 거야.

See if your auto insurance will cover the flood damage. 네 자동차 보험이 침수 피해를 보장하는지 알아봐.

I had to pay 40% of the bill after the car accident. 나는 그 자동차 사고 후에 비용의 40퍼센트를 부담해야 했어.

ChitChat 097

I had my fortune told.
점 봤어.

Kell2013 🔖 have one's fortune told: 점 보다

> I had my fortune told.
> 점 봤어.

Jas
> What for?
> 뭐하러?

Kell2013
> I feel uneasy about the future.
> 미래가 불안해서.

🔖 on a roll: 잘 나가는   **Jas**
> No need. You're on a roll now.
> 뭐하러. 너 요즘 잘 나가잖아.

Kell2013 🔖 job insecurity: 직업의 불안정함 / haunt: 뇌리에서 떠나지 않다, 생각을 멈출 수 없다
> This job insecurity haunts me.
> 직장이 안정적이지 못하단 생각이 떠나질 않아.

Jas
> But you hate being a regular worker.
> 하지만 너 일반 직장 다니기 싫다며.

Kell2013

I know. That's why I choose this but...
그니까. 그래서 이걸 택한 건데...

Jas

You're gonna be all right.
잘 될 거야.

Kell2013

For sure?
정말?

Jas

100 percent sure.
100퍼센트 확신해.

확신을 나타내는 표현

I'm sure he'll make it. 나는 그가 분명 해낼 거라고 확신한다.
It is crystal clear that she's not into me. 그녀가 나한테 관심 없는 건 분명하다.
The final decision is still up in the air. 최종 결정은 아직 내려지지 않았다.
I'm not 100% positive about this. 이것에 대해 100퍼센트 확신하진 못해.
I bet he's going to pass the bar exam. 그가 사법고시에 합격할 거라고 장담해.

ChitChat 098

It cost me an arm and a leg. 과다출혈했어.

백조
Noooooooooo!!!
안~~~~~돼!!!

동분서주
What? What?
뭐? 뭐야?

백조
broken: 고장 난, 망가진
I bought this 3 days ago and it's already broken.
이거 3일 전에 샀는데 벌써 망가졌어.

동분서주
What's "THIS"?
"이거"라니?

백조
on a 12-month (installment) plan: 12개월 할부로
An RB watch I got on a 12-month installment plan!!!
12개월 할부로 산 시계!!!

동분서주
Exchange it or get a refund.
교환하든지 환불해.

 백조

But this was specially ordered and non-returnable.
근데 이건 특별 주문한 거여서 반품이 안돼.

동분서주

Well, then...
그럼, 뭐…

 백조

cost ~ an arm and a leg: ~가 돈을 너무 많이 쓰다, 낭비하다

It cost me an arm and a leg.
과다출혈한 건데.

동분서주

Get it fixed or something.
수선하든지.

 백조

Arrggh. I'm never gonna waste my money again on this stupid kind of thing.
악~~, 이런 바보 같은 것에 다신 돈 낭비 안할 거야.

가격에 관한 표현

It cost me a fortune. 돈 무지 많이 들었어.

That was a steal. 공짜나 다름 없었어.

That store charged me double the price. I got ripped off. 그 가게에서 원래 가격 두 배를 냈어. 바가지 썼어.

The shop offers reasonable prices. 그 가게는 가격이 합리적이야.

ChitChat 099

She's a super haggler.
그녀는 물건 값 흥정의 귀재야.

Kell2013

📢 the other day: 며칠 전에

> I went to Dongdaemun the other day.
> 며칠 전에 동대문 갔어.

📢 Any luck?: (기대치 않게) 좋은 일 있었어? 동분서주

> Any luck?
> 건진 거 있어?

Kell2013

> We got a good bargain.
> 우리 완전 싸게 샀어.

동분서주
> We?
> "우리"라고?

Kell2013

> 천사표 and me.
> 천사표랑 나.

📢 haggler: 흥정을 잘 하는 사람 동분서주

> I heard she's a super haggler.
> 걔가 물건 값 흥정의 귀재라며?

Kell2013

> The rumors are true!
> 소문대로야!

🎵have an eye for ~: ~에 대해 볼 줄 안다, 안목이 있다　동분서주

But does she have an eye for clothing?
근데 옷 고르는 안목도 있던?

Kell2013　🎵I'll say: 정말 그래, 그렇다니까 / *BFF = best friend forever, BF = boyfriend, or best friend

I'll say. She's like a shopper's BFF.
그렇다니까. 쇼퍼의 절친이야.

동분서주

You must feel lucky.
운 좋았구나.

Kell2013

Anyway, I'm ready for spring!
어쨌든 난 봄 준비 완료!

동분서주

Great.
잘됐네.

 쇼핑에 관련된 표현

I'm going on a shopping spree. 나 흥청망청 쇼핑하고 있어.

I shop when I'm bored. 난 심심하면 쇼핑해.

She sure is a smart shopper. 그 여잔 현명하게 쇼핑해.

I normally browse several times before I buy anything. 난 보통 어떤 물건이든 사기 전에 몇 번이고 구경해.

I prefer home shopping because they have a lenient return policy. 관대한 반품제도 때문에 난 홈 쇼핑을 선호해.

I'll have to eat and run.
빨리 먹고 가야 해.

Kell2013

I'm in front of the station. Where r u all?
정류장 앞이야. 다들 어디니?

백조

On my way!
가고 있어!

빈

Me 2. Be there in 5!
나두. 5분 정도면 도착이야!

천사표

Hope you guys don't mind but I'm bringing my husband!
남편 데려가는데 안 불편했음 해.

Tae

♪ **No prob.:** No problem.의 약어, 문제없어, 괜찮아 / **w/o:** without의 약자

No prob! I'll be about 30 min late tho. Start w/o me!
괜찮아! 30분 정도 늦을 것 같은데. 나 빼고 시작해!

빈

Tae, we knew that already. Ur late all the time! Lol
태, 이미 알고 있어. 넌 맨날 늦잖아! ㅋㅋㅋ

Tae

:p
메롱~

겜폐남

Where's the restaurant again??
레스토랑이 어디랬지??

 King_Michael

🎵 heat exhaustion: 일사병

I'm here. Just looking for a place to park.
도착했어. 차 세울 자리 찾고 있는 중야.

🎵 tho: though의 약자 / Sry.: Sorry.의 약자   Jas

Allllllmost there. I'll have to eat and run tho. Sry guys!
거~~~의 다 왔어. 빨리 먹고 가야 하지만. 미안해. 얘들아!

 겜폐남

Found it! Thanks everyone for asking me to be part of your wine tasting group.
찾았다! 너희 와인 테이스팅 동아리에 들어오게 해줘서 다들 고마워.

🎵 on the move: 분주한, 항상 움직이는   동분서주

Always on the move, Jas!
넌 늘 바쁘구나, Jas!

동분서주

겜폐남, glad u can join our meetings. ☺
겜폐남, 우리 모임에 들어와서 반갑다.

More to Talk!

 만남에 관한 표현

I'm running a bit behind. 좀 늦을 거 같아.
Will your girlfriend be able to join? 네 여친도 합류할 수 있을까?
My roommate can't come out tonight. 내 룸메이트는 오늘밤 못 나온대.
Could we change the meeting place? 만날 장소 바꿀 수 있을까?
Let's meet at the coffee shop across the street. 길 건너에 있는 커피숍에서 만나자.
The best way to get there is by taxi. 거기 가는 가장 좋은 방법은 택시야.

Review

Words & Expressions — CHAT 08

ChitChat 087 p 214
What am I? Chopped liver?

inconsistent 일관성이 없는
absent-minded 정신이 딴 데 팔려 있는
You can't have it all. 다 가질 순 없어.
chopped liver 별 볼 일 없는 것 (사람)
like I said 내가 말했다시피
Just name it. 말만 꺼내봐. 이름만 대봐
Don't bite off more than you can chew.
한꺼번에 너무 욕심내지 마.

ChitChat 088 p 216
Cutting food waste helps Korea go greener

trash bag 쓰레기 봉투
separate 분리하다
bag 봉투에 담다
convenience store 편의점
reduce 줄이다
indeed 정말로
do one's part 자기 역할을 하다, 해야 할 임무를 하다
citizen 시민
take out 내어가다
fridge 냉장고
leftover 남은 음식(것)
ingredient 재료
make it habit to ~ ~하는 습관을 들이다

ChitChat 089 p 218
She never throws anything away.

roomie(roommate) 룸메이트
She never throws anything away. 그녀는 도무지 버리질 않아.
overflow 넘치다
hoarder 호더, 병적으로 수집하는 사람
every single day 매일매일
break down 부수다, 허물다
Gimmie(give me) a break. 설마, 그럴 리가.
cluttered with ~ ~으로 엉클어진
neat and tidy 깨끗하고 정리 잘하는
squeaky clean 먼지 하나 없이 깨끗한
put up with 참다, 인내하다

ChitChat 090 p 220
I got caught jaywalking.

get busted 딱 걸리다
jaywalking 무단횡단
I got caught jaywalking. 무단 횡단하다 걸렸어.
straight shooter 법 없이도 살 사람
pay a fine 벌금을 내다
cut some slack 좀 봐주다
warning 경고

CHAT 08

ChitChat 091
Just for kicks.
p 222

reunion 동창회
just for kicks 그냥 재미로
What did I miss? 내가 놓친 것 있어? 뭐 재미있는 것 있어?
ex 구남친, 전남편
expect a baby 곧 아기를 낳을 예정이다
Attaboy! 장하다!
juicy 재미있는
sweetheart 애인
choose A over B B 말고 A를 택하다

ChitChat 092
I'm already regretting it.
p 224

get star-struck (연예인에게) 폭 빠지다
get an autograph 사인 받다
tacky 저속한, 촌스러운
celeb celebrity의 줄인말, 유명 인사
once-in-a-lifetime chance 평생 한번 올까 말까 한 기회
I'm already regretting it. 벌써 후회하고 있어.
Not a chance. 어림 없어.

ChitChat 093
It's like the 7th solid day of rain.
p 226

drizzling 보슬비가 오는
pouring (비가) 퍼붓는

clear up (날이) 개다
It's like the 7th solid day of rain 7일 내리 비가 오는 셈이네.
It's raining cats and dogs. 비가 억수같이 퍼붓는다.
puddle 웅덩이
rainy season 우기
heavy rain 폭우

ChitChat 094
Maybe he has some other issue.
p 228

rug 러그
pricey 비싼
potty training 배변 훈련
issue 문제
Maybe he has some other issue. 뭔가 다른 문제가 있겠지.
ask around 물어보고 다니다, 알아보다

ChitChat 095
Guys, bundle up.
p 230

freezing cold 얼어붙듯이 추운
grab dinner 저녁 먹다
Bundle up, guys! 얘들아, 껴입어.
cozy 아늑한
hang out 만나서 시간 보내다
housework 집안일

CHAT 08

ChitChat 096
Not in a million years.
p 232

get hurt 다치다
Thank goodness. 다행이네
fender bender 접촉 사고
No biggie. 별 거 아니야
stray dog 길 잃은 개
a stroke of luck 운수대통
Not in a million years. 절대 안 해.
car crash 자동차 사고
head-on collision 정면 충돌 사고
auto insurance 자동차 보험

ChitChat 097
I had a fortune told.
p 234

I had my fortune told. 나 점 봤어.
uneasy 불편한
No need. 쓸데없이.
on a roll 잘 나가는
job insecurity 직업 불안정성
haunt 뇌리에서 떠나지 않다
regular worker 일반 직장인
bar exam 사법고시

ChitChat 098
It cost me an arm and a leg.
p 236

broken 고장 난
installment plan 할부
non-returnable 반품이 안되는
It cost me an arm and a leg. 과다 출혈했어.
fix 고치다, 수리하다
That was a steal. 그건 공짜나 다름 없었어.
I got ripped off. 바가지 썼어.
reasonable 합리적인

ChitChat 099
She's a super haggler.
p 238

Any luck? 건진 거 있어?
get a good bargain 좋은 가격에 사다, 완전 싸게 사다
She's a super haggler. 그녀는 물건 값 흥정의 귀재야.
I'll say. 그렇다니까.
shopper's BFF 쇼퍼의 절친
lenient 관대한

ChitChat 100
I'll have to eat and run.
p 240

(I'm) on my way. 가는 중이야.
all the time 늘
I'll have to eat and run. 빨리 먹고 가야 해.
wine tasting 와인 시음
on the move 바쁜, 바쁘게 움직이는
run behind 늦다